FOCUS
ON THE FAMILY®

Tyndale House Publishers, Inc.
Carol Stream, Illinois

ALEX McFARLAND

STAND

diving into God's WORDS

Dedicated to
Princess and Gretel

CONTENTS

INTRODUCTION

As a teenager Earl Greene's goal was to become rich.

By age 21 his net worth was just over $1 million. Intelligent and hardworking, he saw great opportunity in buying and selling real estate around his hometown of Charlotte, North Carolina. By age 26 Earl owned 55 rental houses that generated thousands of dollars in monthly income. He drove around Charlotte in a new Ferrari, which he paid for in cash, and accelerated from success to success.

When he decided to purchase his dream home at age 35, the $650,000 down payment was written from his personal checking account. He owned the largest home in North Carolina's largest county, with a dining and entertainment area that could accommodate a small high school. (Think about that—having a party with 300 guests inside your house!) The house was just one more trophy proving that Earl Greene had made it financially. From his teen years on, Earl had worked hard, and by anyone's standard, he appeared to have it all.

It would be hard not to envy someone like Earl because his life contained everything that we think of as "success." But it all began to crumble early one morning with a knock on the door. Earl recalls: "I woke up, opened the front door of my 13,889-square-foot house—it was a nice front door, by the way—and there stood two men. As one of them flashed a badge at me, I thought, *This is bad, really bad*."

The men at the door were from the U.S. government, and they informed Earl he wouldn't be going in to the office that day; instead he would be coming to spend some time talking to them.

"I was in my pajamas," Earl says. "I asked if I could go change clothes, and they said they'd be happy to wait."

As Earl knew, the government has a lot to say about how housing and lending works. In the course of his real estate transactions, Earl hadn't always followed legal requirements in mortgage lending at his company. Some of Earl's clients had received approval for home loans for which they were unqualified. As a result, Earl received a felony-level conviction for improper real estate practices. Earl was taken away to serve a 55-month sentence in a federal prison. The Ferrari was auctioned off, the mansion was gone, and as for net worth, he was broke. In a matter of weeks, he found himself with nothing.

Earl reflects, "Hard work had made me a millionaire, but greed generated dishonesty, and that eventually made me penniless."

STARTING BACK FROM THE BOTTOM

Sitting alone in an empty jail cell, Earl called for the warden. He asked for a Bible, which the man even-

Psalm 119 fast facts

- 176 verses
- 22 stanzas, called strophes
- each strophe begins with a letter of the Hebrew alphabet
- 8 verses in each strophe
- Longest chapter in the Bible

tually brought, tossing it to him through the bars.

On the cold concrete floor the Bible fell open as Earl knelt to pray. "I poured out my heart to God and honestly said, 'Jesus, I want to know You. This is coming many years overdue, but I give myself back to You. Please be the Lord of my life.'"

When Earl opened his eyes he noticed that his Bible lay open to Psalm 119. "That chapter is near the middle of the Bible," he says. "I guess it just naturally fell open there. I stared down at the text, and what jumped off of the page were the words of verses 9-11."

How can a young man keep his way pure?
    By living according to your word.
I seek you with all my heart;
    do not let me stray from your commands.
I have hidden your word in my heart
    that I might not sin against you.

For the next five years Earl would read and reread Psalm 119. "Let's just say I had plenty of time to work on my spiritual growth," he says, laughing. "In the area of discipleship, I had years of catching up to do. The Bible became my closest friend in that cell—and especially Psalm 119."

Today Earl says that the time in prison was a gift from God. "God brought me to a zero balance financially to help me see that that's where I was spiritually. My tears were not about losing all those things. I was so ashamed for the way that I had forgotten God, pushing Him out of the way as I pursued my dreams. I lost it all to find the Person who gave me everything."

Though reading the entire Bible was part of Earl's daily routine, it was Psalm 119 that impacted him the most. "God used that psalm, I believe with special intent, to comfort me and turn my life around."

Few of us have as dramatic and startling a testimony as Earl Greene, but all of us, in our own ways, have stumbled, have strayed, have forgotten God. All of us need what Psalm 119 provided to Earl: hope, correction, reproof, and instruction.

Every word of the Bible is inspired by God and precious, but I must admit that some parts of it have gripped me more than others. Psalm 119 is one such passage. As my study of Scripture has continued over the years, my fascination with the Psalms, and with Psalm 119 in particular, has turned into genuine love for the chapter's truth and into real appreciation for its beauty and depth. In short, Scripture

The Bible is known by many names!

Among the different versions of Psalm 119, the word "scripture," or God's revelation, is called judgment • Law • precept • statute • command or commandment • testimony • ways • word • ordinance • decree • path • direction • counsel • wise living • instruction • regulation • teaching

is how God has chosen to reveal Himself to us, and Psalm 119 provides important keys to unlocking *all* of Scripture.

This is not merely an academic exercise; it is also a devotional one. The goal is to have a more intimate relationship with the One who gave us Scripture (not to ace a test on Psalm 119). In other words, I want you to know not only the book but the Author as well. That's why we'll begin our journey through Psalm 119 with what this rich chapter has to say about God.

1

GOD

let me tell you about someone i know

Tony works at a paint factory mixing chemicals. He told me about how newbies at the company get broken in.

At the expense of the new employees, workers at the paint factory know exactly how to get a laugh. When a newbie accidentally overfills one of the 55-gallon containers, a veteran at the business will look at the situation and say, "Hurry! We need a drum stretcher!" Tony said that it's hilarious to watch a new recruit frantically search for a nonexistent tool that is supposed to make the container larger.

Another gag goes like this: If a newbie puts too much red in the paint as he mixes it, a more seasoned worker will send him to find the "red extractor." The joke intensifies as the unknowing worker is sent from person to person. All of the veteran workers know to refer the newbie on to someone

Ask "who?" not "why?"

The Bible spends few words on why God does what He does. But the scriptures are full of stories about who God is. It is better to read the scriptures asking "who is God?" before getting locked up asking why? why? why? For example, when King David was still a young shepherd, he heard about the Philistine giant named Goliath, who was taunting the Israelites. David didn't ask God, "why are the

else in the futile search for the red extractor. By the end of this prank, everyone on the shift has gotten a laugh over the newbie's inexperience and naiveté.

Maybe you've been through a similar situation where inexperience and lack of knowledge have resulted in temporary embarrassment. In times like that, help learning the ropes is greatly appreciated.

God knows we're all newbies when it comes to fathoming life and answering the big questions. God neither exploits our lack of knowledge nor passively ignores us as we clamber to find our way in this world. He's not hiding. He's not silent. He's not laughing behind our backs.

God has actively reached out to humanity and to each one of us individually.

YOU CAN KNOW GOD THROUGH THE BIBLE

Every verse of Scripture reveals something of the character of God. Verses that some consider boring,

Philistines beating us up? Why is there war? Why am I the one who has to face this big guy?" Instead he acted on what he knew about God. David had faith that God was powerful, mighty, and would protect His people. Armed with that knowledge in his heart and a slingshot in his hands, David bravely faced the monster Goliath. (For the whole story, see 1 Samuel 17.)

verses with numbers, long lists, or genealogies—even those tell us that GOD is interested in our world. He is alive and at work in the affairs of people.

Specifically what does Psalm 119 tell us about GOD?

Q: Who is God?

A: God is self-existent and sovereign.

Now I don't mean this to be a trick question, but I must tell you that neither the word *self-existent* nor *sovereign* appears anywhere in Psalm 119. However, we know that the writer thinks about GOD this way because he used the word *LORD*. Printers use small caps to signal the use of this unique name. In the Bible, "LORD" is a translation of a special Hebrew word *Jehovah*. *Jehovah* means "eternal GOD" or "self-existent GOD."

The word *sovereign* simply means "king" or "lord." Theologians use the word *sovereignty* to indicate that GOD is in complete control of the universe. In other words, GOD is complete in Himself and is the King over all He has created.

In the face of tragedy and mystery, this is sometimes a difficult principle to grasp. When asking the tough "why?" questions, never forget that GOD is in control. Even though we may not understand Him with our limited comprehension, we can still trust that He has power over the events in our lives.

Verse 91 makes an interesting observation: "Your laws endure to this day, for all things serve you." Did you know that GOD has the power (and wisdom) to orchestrate all things so that they work for His plans and purposes? He does. GOD'S loving, wise control of the universe is such that

A "sovereign" is also a gold British coin, first minted in 1498 for King Henry VII. It has the symbols of the monarchy or "kingship" on it.

He can make every detail—from death to spilled orange juice to a lost fortune—ultimately contribute toward His greater purposes. When we willingly follow His Words, GOD even weaves our mistakes into something beneficial. (Much, much, much more on this in Stand: Seeking the Ways of GOD.)

Q: Who is God?

A: God is holy.

Because GOD is self-existent and sovereign, His very character defines what is right and good or—to use a theological word—"holy." Something—or someone—is *holy* if it is worthy of worship.

This kind of worship is the fall-on-your-face, don't-look-up-or-you-might-be-blinded-with-glory kind of worship (verse 120). It's when you realize you are in the presence of a supernatural, awesome, righteous, pure, unimaginable power.

> *In Old Testament times, when people came into the presence of the holy God, sometimes they took off their sandals (see Exodus 3:5–6 and Joshua 5:15).*

We see this sense of the word throughout Psalm 119. The writer declares GOD'S worthiness every time he addresses GOD as Jehovah. But more than that, the writer directly praises GOD. In verse 164, for example, the writer makes sure there can be no mistake of GOD'S worthiness to be worshiped: "Seven times a day I praise you."

Because GOD is holy, we should approach Him with respect and reverence. When you ask the "why?" questions, remember that the "Who" you are asking is infinitely worthy of all your devotion, honor, and praise.

Q: Who is God?

A: God is loving.

GOD'S love is made plain in Psalm 119. In verse 64 the writer says, "The earth is filled with your love." And it is also interesting that GOD'S love is closely associated with His Law. Let's look at one verse in particular, verse 149: "Hear my voice in accordance with your love; preserve my life, O LORD, according to your laws." Because GOd loves us, He hears our voices and preserves our lives—and He does so according to His laws! GOd'S Law is not a burden; it is a mercy and a protection for us.

You might have noticed that God has favorite numbers: 40, 12, 7, and 3. In the Bible, the number 7 means "complete."

GOd'S instructions are not to make us unhappy; on the contrary, when followed, GOd'S laws provide the ultimate joy and conditions for our success. If you find yourself struggling with obedience and asking, "*Why* does GOd want me to do that?" remember that He has provided the Law for your well-being. GOd has reached out to us with commands because He loves us. One of the best methods for learning about the loving ways of GOd is to understand His Law.

Q: Who is God?

A: God is all-sufficient.

Remember the special Hebrew name *Jehovah* that means "self-existent GOd"? The reality of GOd'S self-existence has many implications. It means, for example, that GOd has the ability to create all that we see from nothing. Because He has that ability—and this is big news—He doesn't need us or our help.

But because He loves us, He allows us to help Him.

When I was growing up, my parents made their living on an egg farm near Greensboro, North Carolina. I would sometimes follow my father around, trying to help with the family business. Often I was more of a hindrance to his work than an asset, but he tolerated it and trained me because he loved me. Eventually I caught on and was a real contributor to the family farm—I learned to keep the place clean, drive the truck, and help my dad with sales. At times I resented the smelly, noisy chickens and hated the work, but today I cherish the memories. I consider the farm one of the truly important and lasting experiences of my life.

In a way, our work for GOD is like my work as a young child on that egg farm. GOD doesn't need us to accomplish His work. In fact, He is all-sufficient. However, He allows us to participate in His ways because it eventually brings His children joy and maturity. That's why Psalm 119:77 says, "Let your

Ex nihilo means "from nothing" in Latin. If you want to sound uber-intelligent, say this often and out loud: "God created the universe and everything in it ex nihilo."

The agnostic says, "No one can know whether or not there is a God—it's impossible." The Christian says, "God has told us who He is; He wants to be known through creation, our conscience, and the Bible."

compassion come to me that I may live, for your law is my delight." GOD'S requirements of us are not for His benefit but for ours; in fact our very lives depend on them.

Because GOD loves us and knows that we depend on Him, He makes Himself known to us in ways we can understand. We will not fully know GOD in this lifetime, but drinking deeply of Psalm 119 can give us an understanding of who GOD is and what He wants us to do. These truths can see us through life's difficult "why?" times.

Who is God according to Psalm 119?

You are my portion, O LORD;
I have promised to obey your words. (verse 57)
You are good, and what you do is good;
teach me your decrees. (verse 68)
Your hands made me and formed me;
give me understanding to learn your commands. (verse 73)
May your unfailing love be my comfort,
according to your promise to your servant. (verse 76)
Your faithfulness continues through all generations;
you established the earth, and it endures. (verse 90)
Yet you are near, O LORD,
and all your commands are true. (verse 151)
Your compassion is great, O LORD;
preserve my life according to your laws. (verse 156)
(See also verses 64, 77, 114, 149, 159, and 168.)

2

SCRIPTURE

the message of psalm 119

We learned in chapter 1 that Psalm 119 tells us about who God is. We learned about God's sovereignty and self-existence, His holiness, love, and sufficiency. But we only scratched the surface. All of God's characteristics are too great for our limited human minds to fully comprehend. One of the measures of God's love is that He does not expect us to know everything about Him before we come to Him. In His mercy, God accepts both the simplest preschooler and the most sophisticated scholar as His "children."

Yet we should not remain children in our faith. We can and should grow spiritually as we learn more and more about who God is. But how?

Let's take a closer look at Psalm 119 and what it tells us about the Words of God, scripture.

Who wrote Psalm 119? Part 1

Though we don't know for sure, some say Ezra, a priest who wrote the Old Testament books of Nehemiah and Ezra (no kidding!). Ezra wrote about a guy named Zerubbabel and the story of when the faithful Jews rebuilt the temple circa 515 B.C. Ezra

PSALM 119, A WAREHOUSE OF WISDOM

According to popular tradition, Israel's kings taught their children to read using Psalm 119 because it is structured around the 22 letters of the Hebrew alphabet. Of course, the kings were also teaching their children a kind of *spiritual* alphabet. The person who learns Psalm 119 will learn to love God's Law and, as a result, will gain much wisdom.

Scripture = the Bible = the Law = God's Word

In fact, of the 176 verses that make up this psalm, 171 refer to Words of God. Clearly, the psalm writer wants us to have not just respect but reverence for scripture. It's reasonable to ask why. As a way of answering that, let me tell a story.

Uh-oh, your kilogram is shrinking!

Try to imagine something you do that does not depend on an honest and true weight or measure. Can you imagine how chaotic life would be if you had to measure every gallon of gas that went into your car, or if you had to synchronize watches with your came to Jerusalem after the temple was built, and he was "a teacher well versed in the Law . . . [and] the hand of the LORD his God was on him" (Ezra 7:6). Ezra was well qualified to write Psalm 119, but some scholars say he lived too late to be the author.

coworkers? What if food manufacturers were free to decide for themselves how heavy an ounce or a pound was? The fact that we have common, agreed-upon standards is a beginning point for virtually all of life's relationships.

In the late 1800s as world commerce grew and scientific advances were being made in countries all over the world, scientists in Europe decided they must agree on the exact weight of a kilogram. They came up with a small weight, composed of the metals platinum and iridium, which equaled one kilogram, and called it the "International Prototype Kilogram" (IPK). This weight was safely stored away. Every 40 years, scientists from various countries were allowed to take this IPK out for examination. In measuring their own countries' kilograms against the ultimate standard for what a kilogram weighs, the captains of science and commerce were able to keep things honest.

But a disturbing thing happened in 2007. During the once-every-40-years inspection of the IPK, it was discovered that after more than one hundred uneventful years, the International Prototype Kilogram

Who wrote Psalm 119? Part 2

some say King David. David was clever and liked
to use acrostics or special structures in his
psalms. David had a habit of using the phrase
"your servant," which is in Psalm 119. And Psalm
119 sounds a lot like Psalm 19, which scholars
say David wrote for sure. Finally there's a whole
bunch of Hebrew words that David liked to use
packed into Psalm 119. All these facts, added to-

didn't weigh a kilogram anymore. The IPK was off.
Not much, but enough for scientists to be alarmed.
Somehow, the weight of the International Prototype Kilogram had changed. The scientific com-
munity was asking, "So how do we *really* know
what the ultimate standard for a kilogram is?"

Theories were tossed about: Had the scientists
in the late 1800s measured incorrectly? Had the
metal object somehow lost some of its mass? Were
our modern computerized scales more accurate
than previous scales? So far, no single answer has
been agreed upon.

THE BIBLE: OUR UNCHANGING STANDARD OF MEASUREMENT, PART 1

The Bible is like that IPK, only better. The Bible is
the standard for goodness, morality, virtue, knowledge about God, and the truth about salvation.

gether with the topic and theme, make some scholars think that David wrote it. Others say that David lived too early to write it. Go figure!

Honestly, the text doesn't say who wrote Psalm 119, and so scholars can only guess. Two things are for sure, though: the author knew God, and we're fortunate to have this amazing poem.

Scripture is our measuring stick, or ultimate standard, by which right is affirmed and wrong is exposed. But the Bible is different from the IPK in two ways: choice and change.

Given by God

The content of the Bible was not chosen by men; it was *given* by God. (See 2 Timothy 3:16-17 and 1 Thessalonians 2:13.) And the message of the Bible doesn't change over time. This Standard of Truth, well, *stands.*

In the last chapter we discovered that an important reason for Scripture is to teach us about who God is. Because God is infinite and transcendent, we could not know Him unless He chose to reveal Himself to us.

Transcendent means "over" and "above" what we can understand. Tell your teachers that their lectures are so clear that they are transcendent. Then watch their faces contort in confusion.

Why is Psalm 119 part of the Bible?

Jesus believed the Old Testament books of the Bible were the standard for truth. He quoted from 24 of the OT books, and He said, "It is easier for heaven and earth to disappear than for the least stroke of a pen to drop out of the Law" (Luke 16:17).

Theologians talk about two kinds of revelation: "general" revelation and "special" revelation. *General revelation* refers to the universe itself and the way it reflects God's character. Psalm 19:1 says, "The heavens declare the glory of God." *Special revelation* most often refers to God's gifts of the Bible and the person of Jesus Himself.

If the words "laws" and "commands" are negative to you, replace them in your mind with the equally applicable words "revelations" and "instructions." Feel better now?

The Bible is a vital part of God's special revelation to us. We did not make it up. God spoke it and "breathed" it as surely as He spoke the universe into existence and breathed life into Adam. As verses 90 and 91 put it, "You established the earth, and it endures. Your laws endure to this day."

Unchanged by people

The Bible is God's precious gift to us. It is the way God chose to reveal Himself to us. Because of that, God has protected that great gift through the ages.

jesus quoted from the psalms at least 12 times. when scholars decided whether a book of the bible was "inspired by god," they used a rule that says, "if it was good enough for jesus, it's good enough for us."

An account of the remarkable faithfulness of men through the ages who have meticulously transcribed the Bible would itself fill many books. Archaeological finds, including the Dead Sea Scrolls (discovered between 1947 and 1956 in 11 caves in Israel), have confirmed the authenticity of the scriptures we have today. Psalm 119 declares the eternal and unchanging nature of God's Words: "Your word, O LORD, is eternal; it stands firm in the heavens" (verse 89).

God Himself has vigorously protected His Word so that we may have knowledge of Him, His Law, and His own unchanging nature.

DON'T OVERLOOK A BURIED TREASURE

Some people assume that since the Bible is such an ancient book, it can't address issues like dating, money, politics, or going to college. Others may have only heard critical comments about the Bible, such as it was altered by power-hungry men or that it's all a bunch of fairy tales. Their only exposure to scripture has been negative. In reality the

Bible is like buried treasure, pure gold that many people walk right past!

This point is illustrated by an incredibly large statue of Buddha that sits outside of a small but famous temple in Bangkok, Thailand. The Temple of the Golden Buddha has some interesting history associated with it. (Your family can check it out on the Internet by doing a search for "Temple of the Golden Buddha" along with "Bangkok.")

In 1957 the statue was going to be moved to a new location. For centuries the statue had been a landmark, with its unmistakable brownish muddy clay exterior. Everyone assumed that this image of the Buddha was made of plaster. When the statue was moved outside by a crane, one of the monks went to check on it during the night. When he showed a flashlight beam on it, he noticed a shiny gleam. He chiseled off some of the plaster, and underneath the crack a bright shiny surface was visible. It turns out that this Buddha was made from tons of pure gold. Historians think that hundreds of years before, Buddhist monks had covered the statue in mud to protect it during a war. By making it look like it was only made of plaster, the monks hoped it would not be stolen.

Just as countless people walked past the statue and for years assumed it had little real value, many today dismiss the Bible as old and worthless. In reality the Words of God are of immeasurable value. Even more so than gold, God's Words are precious and priceless.

The Words of God do these things
for those who follow them

purify (verse 9)

preserve life (verse 25)

strengthen (verse 28)

fulfill biblical promises on a personal level (verse 38)

equip for an answer (verse 42)

comfort (verse 50)

instruct, teach (verses 98-99)

give light, insight (verse 105)

give hope, assurance (verse 114)

sustain (verse 116)

provide peace (verse 165)

deliver (verse 170)

3

RELATIONSHIPS

living for God, living with others

Psalm 119 gives us beautiful insight into how we can have a deep, intimate reLationship with God. His Words show us how we can effectively, and not just superficially, invest in our walk with Jesus and with others. Learning these lessons is the only way to have a truly fulfilling and secure life.

Of course, most of us have to learn these lessons the hard way. I know I did. Let me share a story with you that will help you see what I mean.

FATHER FIGURES

From childhood on up, I worked hard to get noticed. I wanted to get attention.

My dad's attention.

I always wanted my dad to believe in me and to be proud of me. In all fairness, deep down I think that he probably was. I am not writing this to diss my dad. Not at all. He was a solid Christian man, true to my mom and good to his kids. But there was just some kind of gap between us, and nothing I did could bridge it. It would have meant *everything* to me to hear that he believed in me or to know that I was accepted by him.

It really ended up meaning *too much* to me. Many of the things I did growing up—which people near me thought were signs of intelligence or success—were really just my obsessive attempts to earn my dad's favor: graduating from college with honors; earning a master's degree, also with honors; landing prestigious speaking engagements; making money. I told myself that God would be glorified if I superachieved at everything I did. But deep down I knew the truth. I was working more to impress my dad than to honor the Lord.

In 2006 God allowed me to become the president of a seminary and graduate school. That's a pretty big job for a guy who grew up on an egg farm out in the North Carolina countryside.

When I was installed as president, we had a fancy ceremony complete with goofy-looking academic robes and square hats. The school's trustees awarded me an honorary doctor of divinity degree in recognition of "significant accomplishments in ministry and in life."

As I was standing onstage I thought, *My dad must be so proud of me. I'll bet he is so happy right about now.* But a real moment of clarity came just a couple of weeks after the induction ceremony. I asked my dad what he thought about it all, and he told me, "Walking up onto that platform, balancing that hat on your head, and wearing that robe, you looked like . . . a big dumb ape."

Okay, I thought, *maybe my becoming a seminary president hasn't left him terribly impressed.*

I'd be lying if I told you that those words didn't hurt. They did. They didn't change my love for my dad, but I suddenly realized that my quest for his approval had become an idol. Even if I had received his approval, I still would have felt empty. I eventually prayed to Jesus and asked forgiveness for years of misplacing my priorities; I should have been living to please Him, not Dad.

We are to love and honor our parents, family members, friends, spouses, and others around us. However, our ultimate love belongs to Jesus and to no one else. The highest allegiance our hearts can muster belongs to Jesus Christ and to Him alone. That's the only way we can truly feel at peace. Choosing to honor God above all else is the first thing we must do to strengthen our reLationSHip with Him.

AN ETERNAL RELATIONSHIP

Your heart and soul are like precious jewels; don't trust their safekeeping to anyone else but Jesus. Love, serve, risk—but remember that the only place of security and stability is in Christ.

Some reLationSHips we work for in life end

up slipping right through our fingers. When this happens we may become depressed and lonely, even to the point of feeling hopeless. But a Christian can have a reLationship with Jesus that sees us through troubling times and will not slip away even after death. God is invested in us for the long haul.

Psalm 119 encourages us to trust God, His Words, and His faithfulness. These things can never be snatched away from us, and they also form the basis for all other reLationships. The writer cries with confidence, "Your word, O LORD, is eternal; it stands firm in the heavens. Your faithfulness continues through all generations; you established the earth, and it endures" (verses 89-90). A reLationship with God is built on earth, and yet the rewards are experienced throughout all eternity.

False religions offer only philosophy and rules for this lifetime. Christianity offers more: a relationship with the eternal God.

WHAT A RELATIONSHIP WITH GOD OFFERS

Psalm 119 describes a reLationship with God that is give-and-take. If we give obedience (verse 8), God gives protection (verse 93). If we seek understanding (verse 73), He gives us joy (verse 111). If we crave His Words (verse 20), we receive freedom (verse 45). If we do not hesitate to follow Him (verse 60), we can discover intimacy with our Creator (verse 10). If we choose Him (verse 30), He lets us lean on His strength (verses 28, 50, 76, 114, 151, 173). Pretty good deal, huh? And to top it off, the Divine Presence is available 365/24-7.

God offers us acceptance and strength

In the book of Genesis, God's Words tell us that it was "not good" for Adam to be alone. Even though we were created primarily to be in reLationship with God, we were also created to be in reLationship with others: moms, dads, siblings, cousins, grandparents, friends, classmates, husbands, wives.

We have a deep need for intimacy; yet all of us, at some time or another, have felt alienated and alone. Sometimes we try to connect with others in unsatisfying ways. Often we try to build up ourselves so that other people will be attracted to us. We try to be beautiful, strong, smart, trendy, tough, athletic, funny, or cool—anything to be popular and earn admiration.

As a result, unhealthy reLationships often develop. We may have empty reLationships built on gossip, false values, physical attraction, or shallow activities. We accept this as friendship because we don't know anything different.

Another unhealthy strategy is to push aside our loneliness and fill our time with studies, sports, electronic games, or work instead of with people. We may simply keep others at a distance and engage in a hopeless attempt to be completely self-sufficient.

Having a deep reLationship with God helps us get past our fear of rejection and the pressure to be strong and self-reliant. The psalm writer knows that God loves us even though we aren't perfect. We don't have to be beautiful, strong, smart, trendy, tough, athletic, funny, or cool for God to love us. In fact the writer cries to God for security because he is anything but popular. He is continually taunted, mocked, slandered, and persecuted by the people around him (verses 19, 23, 42, 51, 69, 78, 85-86, 95, 110, 141, 161).

Cheesy-but-true saying: God loves us just the way we are. But He loves us too much to let us stay that way.

The writer is humble and dependent on God; he knows he can't stand alone. He asks for understanding and personal strength (verses 27-28). He recognizes his faults and that he needs help to be unselfish, to let go of worthless things, to change, to have good judgment. In his reLationship with God he discovers comfort, life itself, hope, discernment, mercy, peace, and salvation. He comes to God empty but leaves with a secure heart.

Once we have our reLationship with God established, we're equipped to be friends with others.

LIVING WITH OTHERS

Here's a simple checklist to see how your reLationships square with the guidelines in Psalm 119:

- Choose as friends those who follow God's laws (verse 63).
- Encourage other Christians and be encouraged by others (verse 74).
- Support others who live for Jesus and let them support you (verse 79).

Your first priority for friendship and other relationships is to find other Christians whom you can help and who can help you.

Am I saying that you may talk to and be friends with only Christians? NO!

Your consistent Christian character can have tremendous impact on those who don't know Christ. Never underestimate how God might use you to pierce even the toughest hearts. Many believers over the past two thousand years have touched others—and changed history—simply by following Jesus.

Psalm 119 encourages us to be different and to stand out so that God is honored. If you know God's Words, you'll be able to have answers for those who mock Him or His believers (verse 42). You'll know in your heart what is good and what is not (verse 128). When you have the confidence that comes from knowing God, believers and unbelievers alike will see you and look to their own hearts. Those who are seeking God may discover that they need to change because of observing your consistent ways (verses 78-80).

Here's a story that I hope illustrates this point. A friend of mine used to wait on tables in a large restaurant. When it came time for the employees to turn in their 1040 income-tax forms, the other 20 or so servers gathered and agreed to underreport their tip earnings by 40 percent. That way they would all have to pay less to the government, and they would all appear to be earning the same amount of money so the tax auditors wouldn't become suspicious.

My friend didn't join the meeting and decided to report her full income. She thought she could do the right thing simply and quietly, but one day the head waitress cornered her and asked point-blank what amount she was declaring on her tax form. She mumbled the answer, and the head waitress said, "But then the IRS will know all the rest of us are lying. We all have to report the same amount per shift or it won't work."

Blessed are they who keep his statutes (verse 2).

My friend said, "Well, then report the truth, and no one will have anything to worry about."

Afterward, one waitress came up to her and said, "I don't want to get caught because of you, so I'm reporting my full amount. I've always cheated before, but it feels good not to have to worry about getting busted."

Trust me, following the "law," be it from the IRS or God, is so uncommon it will be noticed. It may bring you persecution (ouch!), but it will also win you the respect of those who are open to upholding God's values.

If your reLationship with God is secure, then you have more to offer to others, both Christians and non-Christians.

Dating relationships

I can't have a reLationship chapter in a book for teens that doesn't say something about dating. And at first glance, there's not much about dating in Psalm 119. But let's start with the three principles mentioned in the previous section: Choose godly friends; encourage one another in faith; support other believers.

If you're looking for a boyfriend, a girlfriend, or a "just friends" friendship with someone that could turn into more, please choose someone who has God as number one in his or her life. How can you know if you've found a person like that? Well, that person would be able to talk about God, his or her spiritual life, the Bible, and other spiritual things. You would be helping each other follow God's laws and encouraging each other to become better people who love and serve God.

Learn to take good advice. There's not time in life to make every mistake.

Take a good look at what you can offer someone in the way of spiritual support. If you don't know how to offer someone godly encouragement or feel hesitant to stand up for what you believe, it might be good for you to back away from dating until you are more mature. A good way to spend your teen years is

It's nit-picking, not nitwit picking

If you can't find a dating partner to support you and your spiritual goals, then wait until God brings the right person into your life. Don't go out with just anyone—be picky, extremely picky about character. Girls, you probably spend more time choosing shoes than you do guys. (Sorry to compare you to shoes, guys; I could have said sparkly nail polish or a cute blouse. Somehow shoes seemed the most dignified.) Settle down and wait

to develop your relationship with God and nurture close same-sex friendships. That way you'll avoid some heartache and may be ready for dating later.

And what Christian essay on dating would be complete without mentioning sex? Of course, that discussion wouldn't be totally complete without my admonishing, *"Don't go to bed before you are wed!"* (Now you can say to yourself, *I knew he was going to say that.*) But that's not just Alex McFarland; it's also the Psalm 119 writer, who knows that every good thing comes out of obeying God's Words.

How can a teen keep his or her way pure? By living according to your words (adapted from verse 9).

If you want a secure and fulfilling romantic relationship of any kind, I have to remind you that God's Law says sex outside of the safe context of marriage is spiritually unhealthy and, well, *wrong.* (See Romans 1:24, 29; 13:13; 1 Corinthians 6:13-18;

for the perfect pair. And guys, choose a girl whose heart is right, not merely the outside package. It's like choosing a car. (sorry, girls, but cars are one thing that most guys understand, and they sure don't understand you.) some girls may have a nice paint job, but be confident the engine is sound, or you won't leave the driveway. You may have to wait until you are in your late teens, early 20s, or–gasp!–even longer! But it's worth it.

10:8; Galatians 5:19; Ephesians 5:3; Colossians 3:5; 1 Thessalonians 4:3.)

Any healthy person-to-person relationship needs to be experienced with God's influence. I am in my 40s now and could fill this book with sad stories about friends whose hearts were broken because they failed to follow God's guidelines for love.

If your current dating relationship is veering off into a sexual direction, for your sake, clean it up, even if it means you need to break up. A relationship controlled by sex hormones will disintegrate your relationship with God, and ultimately, having out-of-bounds physical experiences before you are married will hurt both you and your friend.

All good relationships require good communication. In the next chapter let's look at the

foundation of maintaining a reLationship with
God: prayer.

What a relationship with God's law offers

preservation (verses 36–37, 93)

life direction (verse 59)

knowledge and good judgment (verse 66)

comfort (verse 76)

hope (verse 116)

discernment (verse 125)

mercy (verse 132)

peace (verse 165)

salvation and delight (verse 174)

4

PRAYER

talking with God, hearing from God

It's difficult, if nearly impossible, to have a meaningful relationship without communication. In some relationships, communication is more one-sided. For example, when I was growing up, I had a pet goldfish named Goldie. I bonded with that little critter because she gave me communication. It was enough for me that she would come to the glass if I put my face near it. Or when she would swim to the top to nibble on the dried whatchamacallit I gave her as food. I loved Goldie and talked to her every day. I wept when she died and buried her in the backyard next to the hamster, but years later I realized our relationship hadn't been very deep because our communication had been limited. I never truly knew how she felt about me!

Similarly, our relationship with God can only be as good as communication allows. He's done a great deal of communicating—His creation shouts that

He cares for us. The Words He's given us are one long love letter.

We can offer Him prayers in return. Sometimes it seems as if prayer is like talking to Goldie. Does anything really get through? Does He listen? Does He talk back? Can we truly know how God feels about us?

Once again Psalm 119 has the answer. Though the text doesn't use the words pray or prayer, nonetheless the passage speaks volumes on the subject of prayer.

To make my point, I'm going to have to do something drastic and unpalatable. Now don't panic and run around the room, but we are going to have a mini-grammar session. I have to do this to make a dynamic point at the end, so stay with me.

Note that the first verse of Psalm 119 reads like it's talking *about* God—that's called the "third person": "Blessed are they whose ways are blameless, who walk according to the law of the LORD." In the second verse, God is again referred to in the third person; the writer is talking *about* God: "Blessed are they who keep his statutes." Verse 3 continues in the same way: "They do nothing wrong; they walk in his ways."

But notice what happens in verse 4: "*You* have laid down precepts that are to be fully obeyed." Quickly and naturally the writer switches; he is now talking *to* God in the "second person." And Psalm 119 stays more or less in that voice throughout.

Okay, so here's my dynamic point based on the

grammar clue of the "second person" pronoun used throughout the text: Psalm 119 is an extended prayer to God.

Let's look at what God's own Words say about what it means to talk with and hear from Him through prayer. What does He want from us when we pray?

OFFER GOD PRAISE FOR HIS LAW

In verse 12 the writer is enthusiastic: "Praise be to you, O LORD; teach me your decrees." He praises a living God, a God who speaks and teaches through His Words. This chapter is full of this kind of praise. From the beginning (verse 7: "I will praise you with an upright heart as I learn your righteous laws") to the end (verse 164: "Seven times a day I praise you for your righteous laws"), we are led to praise God for His Law.

This verse also suggests that we praise God when we learn His Law and obey His decrees.

You might be thinking: *Why would I praise God for the likes of the Ten Commandments? Why would I praise God for giving us all those rules and regulations, and then some? Seems like that's kind of weird and not a lot of fun.*

Praise is more than singing in church or shouting, "Thank the Lord," when a vending machine accidentally shoots out an extra bottle of Mountain Dew. Praise is uplifting God as a superior, perfect Being.

My response is this: Because following God's Law, learning His ways, and living God's Words are the best ways to know His heart. And being able to know the heart of God is the most valuable privilege in the universe.

And, by the way, praising God's Law is good for us too. When we take time to praise God with our lips, our minds, and our hearts, we reflect on His character and not on our own problems. If we learn to think this way, our minds will gradually transform and begin to reflect the character of God.

OFFER GOD WORSHIP

Worshiping God means wholeheartedly seeking Him—giving yourself to God with a kind of reckless abandon. "Blessed are they who . . . seek him with all their heart," verse 2 teaches us. "I seek you with all my heart," we read in verse 10.

But why do I call this seeking after God, this reckless abandon to God, an act of worship? Because the Bible itself does. Romans 12:1 says to "offer your bodies as living sacrifices, holy and pleasing to God—this is your spiritual act of worship."

So whatever else worship might be, we can say that it is fully submitting ourselves to the Law of God, His Words, and then offering our lives back to Him. Worship, then, is not merely something we do; it is a habit of being before God when we are truly submitted or sold out to Him.

OFFER GOD YOUR PETITIONS

Prayer is praise and worship, but it also includes asking God for things—what is called a *petition*. And because God loves us, He wants us to bring Him our needs. The psalm writer prays for obedience (verse 5), for righteousness (verse 7), for diligence (verse 16), for shelter from scorn and contempt (verse 22), for life (verse 25), for strength (verse 28), for freedom (verse 45)—the list goes on.

A Psalm 119 petition goes way beyond asking for a new iPod. The writer is asking God for a new heart.

But here's the really good news: God does answer prayers. He answers prayers because He loves us. He answers prayers because He is teaching us to ask rightly, and when we do so, the answered prayers become an encouragement and a signpost on our spiritual journey. He answers prayers because it pleases Him to do so; it brings glory to Himself.

Ask for open eyes

When we pray, what should we ask God for? In verse 18 the psalm writer asks God to "open my eyes that I may see wonderful things in your law." There are places where God's Words are so plain and explicit that the meaning is unmistakable, even to a child. But not all of Scripture is that way. Beautiful, complex, and mysterious ideas are not always immediately accessible.

It's as if we're in kindergarten and the teacher asks us to fill in a dot-to-dot drawing. As we learn to count, we move our pencils from number one to two, then three to four. Slowly the picture reveals itself. God's Words are sometimes that way for us. While we are first learning, we must fill in the "dots" one by one to see the "picture" God is presenting.

Also, God is infinite, and our understanding is finite. The learning process requires us to wrestle with God's Words. As we do, we see "wonderful things" in His Law, and our eyes are also open to see His character as well as the true state of the world. We should pray that God will open our eyes to truths and realities that might be beyond our current experience but not beyond our understanding.

Ask for safety from scorn and contempt

Have you ever known people who have such integrity that even when you disagreed with them, you carefully considered their point of view? You thought, *Maybe they're right and I'm wrong.* Such a person is someone like the person described in verse 22: a person free from "scorn and contempt." But how do you get to be such a person? By keeping God's statutes.

Of course, Jesus was such a man. One of the most interesting verses in all of Scripture is the description of the young Jesus, who—Luke 2:52 says— "grew in wisdom and stature." But Luke says more. Jesus also grew in "favor with God and men."

Don't have a heart attack

In Luke 18:1 Jesus tells the disciples a parable to show them to "always pray and not give up." The Greek word for "not give up" can be translated "don't lose heart" or "do not despair." It can also mean "don't have a heart attack." So if you're in a position where panic and desperation preside, pray. Even if you're going into cardiac arrest, the Bible says that you should pray.

Ask for obedience

Obedience to God's Law won't earn you salvation. However, obedience to His Law is both something God desires for us and something we will desire as we grow closer to Him. I don't know about you, but there are some things I pray for that I'm not sure God wants me to have—because my prayers are too often selfish. But when you pray to be obedient to what God has shown you, you can be sure that you are praying a prayer that is absolutely in the center of God's will for your life. Pray for obedience. Pray for the strength to be obedient in difficult situations. Pray that your Christian brothers and sisters will be obedient to God's Law. Pray, even, that they will obediently and lovingly chastise you when you are disobedient!

Ask for unfailing love

It may seem strange or illogical to ask for God's unfailing love (see verse 41). After all, if it is unfailing, why would we need to pray for it? Won't it always be there whether we pray for it or not? That's sort of like praying, "God, please don't repeal gravity today. Please don't let me fly off into space!"

This verse gets at the heart of why we pray. We pray because God asks us to, because it brings Him glory, and because prayer matures us. God's love is unfailing, but we often fail to remember it. By having this prayer ever on our lips and in our minds, we have one of God's fundamental attributes— His love—constantly before us.

Ask from the heart

You may be asking, "Is it okay to pray for other things, like help deciding on a career, that my dad gets a job, or that my friend with leukemia is healed?" Of course, tell God everything that's on your heart—even if you want the latest electronic gadget or a new skateboard. If you include prayers like the ones the psalm writer prayed, you will be better equipped to live out God's Words.

God is much more than a cosmic ATM machine that doles out gifts to change your physical world. He wants to change your spiritual world, your eternal savings account.

So, according to the psalm writer, does God answer our prayers? Is God's response better than a goldfish's gape-mouthed, vacant expression? Yes! In almost every case, the psalm writer acknowledges that the answer to our prayers is finding more of God: "You are my portion, O LORD; I have promised to obey your words" (verse 57). When we obey God's Words, we find that we have our "portion," what we need. Indeed, that's a key insight of Psalm 119: God answers our prayers through our acts of obedience.

Cries that get answers

Praise be to you, O LORD;
teach me your decrees. (verse 12)
Do good to your servant, and I will live;
I will obey your word. (verse 17)
Open my eyes that I may see
wonderful things in your law. (verse 18)
I am a stranger on earth;
do not hide your commands from me. (verse 19)
Remove from me scorn and contempt,
for I keep your statutes. (verse 22)
May your unfailing love come to me, O LORD,
your salvation according to your promise. (verse 41)

5

TRUTH

right, wrong, and everyday living

None of us can earn a way into heaven. In chapter 1, when we discussed what Psalm 119 tells us about the nature of God, we said that God is holy, or a supernatural, awesome, righteous, pure, unimaginable power. Our ability to have a relationship with Him—called "salvation"—is 100 percent His reaching down to us and 0 percent our reaching up to Him.

Nonetheless, God wants us to reach out to Him. In fact, Psalm 119 is full of passages that say believing the right things is good. That's the first step of salvation. But to be close to God in an intimate relationship, we have to *do* the right things too. Verse 5 sums it

Fancy word alert: Orthodoxy is "believing the right things about God." Orthopraxy is "doing the right things." (Orthodontics is having the right teeth!)

up, "Oh, that my ways were steadfast in obeying your decrees!"

Why is that? Why would God be so concerned about what we do when we can't do anything to earn salvation? To help answer that question, let me tell you another story.

THE BIBLE: OUR UNCHANGING STANDARD OF MEASUREMENT, PART 2

One morning a man ran into a railway station, afraid that he had missed the train he was supposed to be on. Out of breath, he panted out a question to the ticket agent: "What time does the 8:01 morning train leave?"

"Umm . . . at 8:01."

The man answered, "Well, my watch says it is 7:59. The clock outside the bank says it is 7:57, but the clock on the wall here in the station says it is 8:03."

The ticket agent merely stared at him.

Desperately the man asked, "Which should I go by?"

"You can go by any clock you want," said the agent. "But you can't go by the 8:01 train, because it just left."

Many people today have differing ideas about what is right or wrong, true or false. Though vitally significant, the list of life's truly important questions is fairly short. They include questions like this: Where did we come from? Why am I here? Where is the world headed? What should I do with my life? What happens after death? Who is God? What does God want from me?

The list of probing questions may be brief, but there is no shortage of answers. Ask 10 different people any of the previous questions, and you're likely to get about two dozen different answers! But the responses will have one thing in common: Unless the person speaks from a Christian perspective, the answer will be little more than personal *opinion,* which include preferences, speculation, and bias. We all have opinions, we all hold them about certain things, and popular ideas change like the wind. If it weren't for the fact that God has given us His Words, we simply wouldn't have solid answers about truth. God's Words are His opinion; His opinion is the only one that equals the plain and simple truth.

Absolute truth is what is always true for all people, no matter the time, place, or a person's beliefs. For example, the fact that the earth is round was not wiped away by seventeenth-century "scientists" who said it was flat.

But—thank God—He has given us His Words! Psalm 119 has a great deal to say about morality, or "truthful living." We'll focus on two key ideas from this psalm: moral purity and spiritual consistency. But first, let's look more at the concept of absolute truth.

HYPOCRISY AND ABSOLUTE TRUTH

In my work as a Christian apologist, I often speak with atheists, agnostics, doubters, and even some Christians who have questions about Christianity. Many people say that they won't become believers in Jesus because Christians are hypocrites. They say Christians do not practice what they preach. They then conclude that Christianity must not work. While their observations are (sadly) correct, their logic is not. Christian truth is not wiped away by the failure of Christians. Jesus Christ died on the cross, was buried in a tomb, and after three days rose again. That basic Christian truth has nothing to do with how I, you, the pastor's son, or anyone else acts.

Actually, hypocrisy is a proof that Christianity is true.

An apologist is not someone who keeps saying, "I'm sorry. I'm sorry." Apologetics means "defense." An apologist defends the Bible, Christian beliefs, and Christ's resurrection.

Christian hypocrisy, mistakes, and sin demonstrate the need of humankind for a Savior; just as Romans 3:23 says, "All have sinned and fall short of the glory of God."

Ironically, many people who object to Christianity on the basis of hypocrites are unknowingly proving that moral truth exists. Think about it—who says hypocrisy is "wrong"? Who made that moral judg-

The truth about truth

It's difficult—I would say impossible—to completely refute the idea that truth and morality do not exist. For example, the very statement "truth does not exist" contradicts itself! Said another way, when someone tells me there is no such thing as truth, I always ask: Are you sure? If they are sure there is no such thing as truth, then that statement becomes his or her truth. Don't you see? Arguing against truth is illogical.

ment? Even the concept of the word *hypocrite* suggests there are right and wrong ways to act. This concept of right and wrong behavior is a fundamental Christian truth.

Hypocrisy is wrong, and if Christians behaved better, our witness in the world would certainly be more powerful, and Christ would have a better reputation. But, again, when Christians behave badly, that doesn't prove that Christianity is not true. Hypocrisy simply means that not all Christians act in faith at all times.

Hypocrisy is not the real issue. Neither is the question "Does truth exist?" The real question is "Whose truth will I believe? God's truth or some temporary, man-made truth?"

If you decide to follow God's truth, then Psalm 119 is a great place to start, and in this chapter we discover two moral principles mentioned or alluded to again and again: moral purity and spiritual consistency.

MORAL PURITY AND SPIRITUAL CONSISTENCY

One of the most famous verses in all of Scripture is Psalm 119:9: "How can a young man keep his way pure? By living according to your word." This verse is often, and rightly, used to describe how we can overcome temptation. But because the verse is specifically directed to a "young man," the implication is that even though the following temptations are common to all people, too often they define the lives of young men: sexual temptation, arrogance, carelessness, and pride. In the words of a popular country song, young men too often think of themselves as "ten feet tall and bulletproof."

But there is more to this psalm, and this verse, than just a specific instruction to a specific young man. The question posed by verse 9 actually goes to the heart of the gospel. How can we, sinners, come into the presence of a holy God? The answer is, again, simple but not easy: "By living according to your word."

Obeying God is not a one-time thing. Psalm 119 talks about it as a constant, daily, even minute-by-minute renewing of our minds and strength.

Here's an example to show you what I mean.

Ever since I was a boy, I've been a guitar junky. My favorite brand is Rickenbacker, the preferred instrument of the Beach Boys and the Beatles. Ricks have been my passion since I was 11. Even after I became a Christian, I'd justify buying them by saying, "Well, I use them at praise bands." At one time I owned five Rickenbackers—any one of the guitars was worth more than my car. In the 1980s I was fortunate to purchase a Rickenbacker 360/12 BWB; only 200 were made. I was in heaven owning this rare, coveted guitar. It was a prized possession. I felt like Charlie in *Charlie and the Chocolate Factory* when he won a golden ticket.

Enter God.

In 1989 I sold that guitar to pay tuition for my master's degree in apologetics from Liberty University. I knew I was called to defend the gospel, and the sale was well worth the sacrifice. But it was still difficult turning over that guitar to a dealer in Winston-Salem, North Carolina.

Today I'm a reforming guitar junky; I don't buy and sell as I used to. But occasionally I check eBay auctions to see what's available. One day last year I saw a special guitar for sale—yes, a rare and coveted 360/12 BWB. And it wasn't just any old rare and coveted 360/12 BWB. It was mine!

I could tell it was mine by the hand-painted case. I could tell it was mine by the scratches on the pick guard. I could tell it was mine by the small indentation in the velvet case lining next to the nickel-silver tuning keys. It was mine by sentimental rights, and it was mine by the laws of commerce—I had the money to pay for it. The guitar was mine, and I had 15 minutes left to buy it.

I even told myself it would make a great story to

tell people how God had brought back to me what I had sacrificed for Him. I could all but feel that guitar in my hands, could hear it playing old Beach Boys tunes. A German shepherd in front of a T-bone steak couldn't have been more excited than I was to buy that guitar. But for some reason I didn't click on the Buy-It-Now button as the seconds and then the minutes ticked away.

After the auction ended I felt a great spiritual peace. I had resisted the ultimate guitar junky temptation for me. I had passed some sort of spiritual test. I realized I had reached a level of self-control that would have been unimaginable to me when I was a teen. But I hadn't gotten there overnight. It had taken more than 20 years to develop a different truth system, a day-by-day commitment to spiritual values that say there's more to life than owning guitars.

Maintaining spiritual consistency takes more than praying a "sinner's prayer" and then continuing to live as before. Believers must use the Words of God as an essential tool for resisting temptation and for maintaining moral purity, spiritual consistency, and a commitment to truth. "I have hidden your word in my heart that I might not sin against you" (verse 11).

Believe it or not, when I was a teen and pursuing guitars and everything else that I wanted, I was unhappy deep down inside. After I gave up my life to Christ and let go of the things I wanted, I have become more and more joyful and at peace in my spirit. How can you find some of that same happiness? Let's take a look at chapter 6.

More Psalm 119 on moral purity and self-discipline

I have considered my ways
and have turned my steps to your statutes. (verse 59)
I will hasten and not delay
to obey your commands. (verse 60)
Before I was afflicted I went astray,
but now I obey your word. (verse 67)
I rise before dawn and cry for help;
I have put my hope in your word. (verse 147)
My eyes stay open through the watches of the night,
that I may meditate on your promises. (verse 148)
May my lips overflow with praise,
for you teach me your decrees. (verse 171)
May my tongue sing of your word,
for all your commands are righteous. (verse 172)
I have strayed like a lost sheep.
Seek your servant,
for I have not forgotten your commands. (verse 176)

6

HAPPINESS

what it takes to find it

I know the formula for happiness. It has nothing to do with clear skin, a great girlfriend or boyfriend, popularity, money, cool clothes, or winning the school football game. You can't buy it, sell it, steal it, or hoard it. It's free, yours for the taking. It's a very simple formula, but not an easy one. Plus, it's been in plain sight for centuries.

The first two verses of Psalm 119 offer this advice for those seeking happiness: "[Happy] are they whose ways are blameless, who walk according to the law of the LORD. [Happy] are they who keep his statutes and seek him with all their heart."

Blessed = Favored = Happy = Joyful

The only four things necessary for happiness are a blameless way, walking according to the Law of the Lord, keeping His statutes, and seeking Him wholeheartedly.

Yeah, right! Can any of us honestly say that we do all of these things all of the time? I know I can't. Yet I want to be happy all the time.

So, is this some sort of trick from God? We desire happiness but can never attain it?

Happiness isn't avoiding problems; it's having the faith to overcome them.

No! Let's look at the rest of the chapter to find out how to convert these four concepts into day-to-day happiness.

NO. 1: A BLAMELESS WAY

Remember, without God's grace it is impossible for us to be truly blameless. But if we have trusted Christ for the forgiveness of sins, we are—in God's eyes—totally blameless.

You may read Bible stories and marvel at how God worked through such men as Moses, David, and Paul. Quickly that marvel may turn to shame because you remember your own past and history of failed faith. You may have thought what I have thought: *God can't use me. There is too much sin in my life. I haven't walked a blameless way. These stories about Moses, David, and Paul are fantastic, but I'm no Moses!*

You're right. You are no Moses.

Moses was a murderer who ran from God for 80 years, and even then it took a burning bush to get his attention. David, too, was a murderer, and that's not counting his adultery with Bathsheba. Paul (aka Saul) may not have committed the act of murder, but he guarded the cloaks of those who stoned the faithful Stephen. So we'll lessen the charge to accessory to murder.

In all three cases God wiped these heinous sins away. Because of these men's complete abandonment to God's grace and the truth of Scripture, God deemed them blameless and used them to change the history of humankind.

Is your way blameless? It can be. Simply trust Christ to take your sin away. Knowing that you are forgiven is the foundation of all kinds of lasting happiness. It also gives you the confidence to serve the Lord with as much passion as Moses, David, and Paul.

NO. 2: WALKING ACCORDING TO THE LAW, AND NO 3: KEEPING HIS STATUTES

Okay, so now you're blameless. What comes next?

Something wonderful and mysterious happens when we turn from our sins and turn our lives over to God. We are empowered by God's Spirit to live at a level previously impossible. Jesus puts it simply, unmistakably: "With God all things are possible" (Matthew 19:26).

I want to be clear that I'm not talking about a legalistic, works-based, I-can-please-God-by-going-to-church-and-never-ever-cursing plan. I'm talking about complete submission to God. The sixteenth-century church reformer Martin Luther put it this way: "Love God and do as you please." That may sound glib, but it actually reflects great wisdom. If you truly love God, nothing will please you that will not also please God.

So when verse 1 tells us that we should "walk according to the law of the LORD," it is a life-changing, awesome concept that can only be done through the supernatural work of God's love in your life.

And when we encounter a phrase such as "Blessed are they who keep His statutes," we should remember that the key word here is *His*. God has blessed and anointed His Words. He has made many promises that are specific to Scripture. In fact, this very verse is one of those promises. If you keep His statutes, you will be blessed or happy.

If you want to be happy, try looking upward and outward instead of inward. While you are distracted, happiness just might sneak up and conk you on the head.

What a marvelous promise.

And that brings us to the next idea in our quest for full and true happiness.

NO. 4: SEEKING HIM WITH ALL YOUR HEART

Many Christians and non-Christians alike try to offer a list of dos and don'ts in exchange for a sub-

But I digress . . .

This has nothing to do with the theme of this chapter, but I just can't resist pointing out evidence for Jesus' being part of the Trinity. The answer Jesus gave the rich young ruler is interesting because He accepted the man's description of Him as "good." Don't you see? By saying that "no one is good—except God alone," Jesus is in reality acknowledging that He is God. Goodness gracious!

missive heart that obeys God's Spirit. Mere checklist compliance with the Law is not what God desires. It's like the kid who took two cookies from the cookie jar. His mother noticed the cookie jar out of place and asked him, "Did you take a cookie?" The kid replied, "No, ma'am, I didn't take *a* cookie." In fact, he had taken *two* cookies. The kid had given an accurate answer, but he had not told the truth. The child got an extra cookie, but he lost God's blessing, and most likely his mother's trust.

Jesus once encountered a man who tried to play that game with him. The rich young man came to Jesus, fell on his knees, and said, "Good teacher . . . what must I do to inherit eternal life?"

Jesus responded: "Why do you call me good?. . . No one is good—except God alone. You know the commandments: 'Do not murder, do not commit adultery, do not steal, do not give false testimony, do not defraud, honor your father and mother.' "

We see that Jesus was in fact affirming the Old Testament Law. Some Christians today say that because we live in the "age of grace," the time after the life, death, and resurrection of Jesus, we do not need to pay attention to the Law. Jesus' answer to the rich young ruler suggests that is not true. The Law still mattered to Jesus.

In fact, Jesus took it a step further. The man said, "All these I have kept since I was a boy."

Then something happened that was so remarkable I want to use the exact words:

> Jesus looked at him and loved him. "One thing you lack," he said. "Go, sell everything you have and give to the poor, and you will have treasure in heaven. Then come, follow me."
> At this the man's face fell. He went away sad, because he had great wealth. (Mark 10:21-22)

Once again this answer is rich in meaning, as are all of the Words of Jesus. Here, Jesus was vitally concerned about the man's keeping God's Law—in fact, that's the way Jesus "loved" this man. Jesus asked all these questions in part to expose the fact that the man had *not* kept all of God's Law. With that one question, Jesus showed that the man was lying, that he coveted, and that he idolized wealth. This man who professed to have obeyed the Law from his youth was in violation of at least three of the Ten Commandments!

But there's more to this story. Jesus was really asking the man, "Are you willing to give up everything for me?" If you are, you will find true happiness. If not, like the rich young ruler, you will walk away from Jesus with a sad heart.

Psalm 119 on rejoicing in His Words

Blessed are they who keep his statutes
and seek him with all their heart. (verse 2)
I delight in your commands
because I love them. (verse 47)
Your decrees are the theme of my song
wherever I lodge. (verse 54)
Oh, how I love your law!
I meditate on it all day long. (verse 97)
Your statutes are my heritage forever;
they are the joy of my heart. (verse 111)
I rejoice in your promise
like one who finds great spoil. (verse 162)
I long for your salvation, O Lord,
and your law is my delight. (verse 174)

7

BLESSINGS

there are some strings attached

What's in it for me?

That's the way the world thinks. The value of virtually everything in life is measured by that question. The value of an education is measured by how much money it allows you to make when you get out of school. The effectiveness of government is measured by what it does for us. Even marriage is measured by how satisfied it makes us—emotionally, sexually, or financially.

It wasn't always so. There was a time when wise men and women knew that the true blessings in life came from a life of service. For example, George Washington said, "Happiness and moral duty are inseparably connected." Maybe the first U.S. president knew what Jesus was talking about when He said, "For even the Son of Man did not come to be served, but to serve, and to give his life as a ransom for many" (Mark 10:45).

So if being bLessed by God is not getting what I want when I want it, what does it truly mean to be bLessed, to be happy in the sense that Psalm 119 and the rest of Scripture mean?

On the road to duty you often stumble upon happiness.

Let's focus on a few of the main bLessings that Psalm 119 tells us will come to those who "walk according to the law of the LORD" and who "seek him with all their heart."

THE BLESSING OF FREEDOM

Psalm 119 talks about freedom in the context of oppression. The psalmist's "persecutors" (verse 84), "evildoers" (verse 115), and "oppressors" (verse 121) seem to surround him. But the psalmist experiences freedom because he will "not turn from your law" (verse 51).

Indeed, the idea of freedom is one of the great themes of Scripture. In Galatians 5:1, Paul wrote, "It is for freedom that Christ has set us free." But what does that mean? It sounds like a bit of double-talk, but it's not. God desires us to be free—completely free. He desires us to be free from economic and political bondage, but more than that, He wants us to be free from sin and death.

From time to time I hear people ask, "How could a loving God allow evil in the world?" You could make a powerful answer to that question by simply saying this: "God wants us to be free. *Completely* free." We even have the freedom to choose evil, to do wrong. Without this freedom to choose, God's grace would be cheap, and our obedience would be meaningless.

But when we choose well, there is great joy. We have an inkling of the world to come, when in complete freedom we will worship God forever.

THE BLESSING OF LIGHT

Light as a symbol for truth is one of the recurring ideas in Scripture and one of our most valuable blessings. In the beginning "God said, 'Let there be light,' " and He called the light "good" (Genesis 1:3-4). In the gospels Jesus called Himself the "light of the world" (John 8:12). We are told, "Let your light shine before men, that they may see your good deeds and praise your Father in heaven" (Matthew 5:16).

Psalm 119 tells us that God's Words are a "light" to our "path" (verse 105). We read in verse 130 that "the unfolding of your words gives light."

These verses represent a great power when we understand the true nature of light. First of all, light destroys darkness. Darkness is not a thing itself; rather, darkness is the absence of light. Darkness has no power over light. The smallest candle has power over the most complete darkness. And the most complete and utter darkness cannot put out a light. In the battle of light over darkness, light always wins.

Another blessing of light is that it illuminates. That may seem obvious, but it is an important idea.

Melancholy quote alert: Comfort the child who fears the darkness, but pity the man who fears the light.

Where there is light, other things that were previously hidden in the darkness become visible. When we are told that God's Words are a "light to our path," we are being given a great gift. We have the secret of how we can confidently walk without stumbling in a world that often seems dark, confusing, and committed to making us fall.

Light also has an attractive force. When we look up at the sky at night, do we look at the blackness or at the stars? Our eyes are naturally drawn to the stars. Light a candle in a dark and empty wood, and you'll soon discover moths flying all around it.

God's Words are a light. When we are filled with God's truth, the truth of God's Words, we are a light to a dark world, a blessing to a lost people.

THE BLESSING OF COMFORT

We often hear expressions such as "no pain, no gain." Some motivational speakers and leaders talk about personal growth resulting from being stretched or forced out of your comfort zone. Well, when you're out of your comfort zone, expect God to draw you into His comfort zone. Jesus promised, "Blessed are those who mourn, for they will be comforted" (Matthew 5:4).

Will was 13 years old when his parents split up. Shortly before their divorce, he had invited Christ into his life while attending a church function. From that point on, Will knew what it meant to have the peace that comes from a relationship with Jesus Christ. But Will had never known a time when his home life was peaceful. His father, though a Christian, had trouble getting and keeping a decent job. His mother was an alcoholic.

"My parents argued constantly," Will remembers. "When Mom was drinking, things could get pretty brutal. My parents didn't intentionally try to hurt us, but my brother, two sisters, and I suffered from a home life that on most days was just about unbearable."

The Bible's power to provide comfort and assurance is vividly illustrated in Will's testimony: "Reading my Bible had such a calming effect on me. I remember reading about God's love, God's power, God's goodness, and that He had a plan for my life. Growing up was not easy, but over and over, verses would stick in my mind and give me comfort. My hurt began to turn to love for my parents, which led me to pray for them."

Maybe you can relate to Will's story. It reminds me of verse 52 of Psalm 119: "I remember your ancient laws, O LORD, and I find comfort in them."

Don't miss your blessings!

In his book "Eat Mor Chikin: Inspire More People," Truett Cathy, the founder of the restaurant chain Chick-fil-A, tells a story about a young man he was mentoring. Cathy would meet with the young man periodically, giving him advice and providing him with opportunities. Sometimes Cathy bought him clothes or books to help him advance on his way.

But at a certain point in the relationship, Cathy sensed that the young man was becoming too complacent, perhaps even lazy. "He needed a car," Cathy wrote, "and I wanted to help him. More than a car, though, he needed direction."

So Cathy sent the young man a series of sermon tapes that he thought would help provide that direction. "As a reward for listening to the tapes, I was going to give him the car he wanted," Cathy wrote. "But I didn't tell him that." Instead,

THE BLESSING OF WISDOM

What is wisdom? A simple answer is having a God's-eye view of the world. In other words, it is seeing things from God's perspective. But what does that mean? What's the difference between God's perspective and a human's perspective?

The primary difference is that God is not limited by either time or space. That's part of what is meant when we call God "eternal" and "transcendent" (see chapter 1). We, on the other hand, are limited by time and space, and that influences our thinking and the decisions we make.

We humans have an unfortunate tendency to

on the last tape in the series, cathy had recorded over the preacher's message, telling his friend that "the keys to his car were waiting for him in atlanta."

over the next few weeks, cathy would call his young friend and ask about the tapes, but after weeks had gone by, cathy said he would like his tapes returned so he could give them to someone else who might enjoy them. the young man did eventually bring the tapes back, and cathy said, "while he sat in my office, we listened to the last tape together, both of us terribly sad because of his missed opportunity."

according to cathy, this incident was "a powerful lesson—one that neither he nor I will forget. to receive a blessing, we often have to take action first."

seek here-and-now gratification rather than to seek eternal blessings. True wisdom sees things from God's perspective. True wisdom listens to God's voice. Developing true wisdom in our lives is what the study of and obedience to God's Law is all about.

CONDITIONS OF GODLINESS

God made us in His image, but our sin has marred that beautiful model. God's goals are to restore that holy image in us and restore our relationship with Him like it was in the Garden of Eden.

We can't earn our way to that restoration—Jesus

is the only One who could pay our sin penalty, and praise God that He did! Theologians call that "justification." But justification is not the end of the Christian life. It is the beginning. The process of sanctification comes next, and it is a lifelong process. The word *sanctify* means to "set apart for special use." And as that definition suggests, even though there is nothing we can do to cause our own justification, there is much we can do to participate in our own sanctification. Or, as Christian speaker Bob Shank has said, "Salvation has nothing to do with works, but living the Christian life has everything to do with getting to work."

So what obligations do we have, according to Psalm 119? Let's look at a few of them.

Obedience

The words *obey* or *obedience* appear more than a dozen times in Psalm 119. Knowing God's Words is a good thing, but obeying God's Words is the real goal. Consider, for example, the Great Commission of Matthew 28:16-20, one of the most famous passages in the New Testament. The verses say to do more than to preach the gospel or to make converts. This passage says to teach "everything" Jesus commanded us. That's a tall order! And not just to "teach" but to "teach them to obey." In other words, a preacher is not done until his hearers are obeying God's Words! Obedience is a desired outcome of the Christian life.

Discipline

Is there something you are good at? Sports? Music? Art? My guess is that you spent long hours, weeks, and even years mastering that activity. It's likely you love that activity. That's probably what got you involved in the first place.

But if you are really good at something, there are times when you've had to work hard to get better.

> *You can either enjoy the pain of discipline today or the pain of being unprepared tomorrow. The choice is yours.*

I've enjoyed playing the guitar since I was about seven. Over the years I suppose I've gotten fairly good at it. But I find that if I just play the same songs and chords over and over again, I don't get any better. Years ago a professional musician counseled me to "get with guys who will force you to play just beyond yourself." So now I purposely try to jam with musicians who are better than I am. I have to push myself to play things I've never played before or do exercises that are boring but strengthen my fingers. The not-so-fun stuff ultimately allows me to have more fun and derive greater satisfaction from my music.

Your Christian walk is like that. We all want to lift our heads with spiritual pride, but few of us want to spend time on our knees. Many of us want to be known for our knowledge of the Bible, but few of us want to study. Discipline is the key to the

mature spiritual life and full participation in God's
bLessings for us.

Perseverance

In our fast-food, instant-everything culture, perse-
verance is a lost virtue. But it is important for us
to remember that God is more interested in developing our character than giving us what we want,
when we want it. Sometimes even when we ask for
the right things in the right way, God doesn't immediately answer our prayers because we are not
ready to receive the answer.

Kurt Warner's life is a clear example of this principle. As a young man he wanted more than anything to play professional football. But he went to a
college that was not a football powerhouse and
rode the bench until his senior year. He was cut by
one pro team and had to take a job as a stocker in a
grocery store to earn a living. Finally he was offered
a tryout by another team, but right before the ap-
pointment, he was bit by a venomous spider and
had to miss the tryout!

All of these setbacks would have been reasons
to assume that a career in football just wasn't
meant to be. But Warner persevered, taking a job
in football wherever he could. That meant he played
arena football in the United States and pro football
in Europe before finally getting the call by an NFL
team.

During that time in the trenches, however, he
met his future wife, and his relationship with God

deepened. Warner ultimately became one of the top NFL quarterbacks of all time. He won the NFL Most Valuable Player (MVP) award twice, was named 1999 Super Bowl MVP, and he is considered by many a sure bet for the NFL's Hall of Fame. But today Warner says that it was those years outside of the public limelight that prepared him to handle what came next. He believes God allowed him to go through those tough years so that the things that are now the most important to him—faith and family—could take strong root in his life.

Because Warner persevered, he ultimately was rewarded with great success. If at any point he had given up, the football prizes would have been forever lost. But more important than that, if he had not persevered, the character qualities that now make him a respected and happy man, husband, and father would not have fully developed either.

THE PRICE AND THE PRIZE

In life, especially in our spiritual lives, you can count on this principle: Before any prize comes a price.

Remember what I wrote earlier in the chapter: You can't earn your way into heaven. Jesus paid that price. Your salvation, your justification before a holy and just God, has been paid in full. But your sanctification is ongoing, and it requires your participation. It will determine your personal joy and happiness. It will determine your openness and availability to God so that you can do His works. It is my prayer that by following the wisdom of Psalm 119, your joy and your usefulness to the kingdom will be full and complete.

What's obedience got to offer me?

I remember your ancient laws, O Lord,
and I find comfort in them. (verse 52)
In the night I remember your name, O Lord,
and I will keep your law. (verse 55)
This has been my practice:
I obey your precepts. (verse 56)
Do good to your servant
according to your word, O Lord. (verse 65)
Your commands make me wiser than my enemies,
for they are ever with me. (verse 98)
I have more insight than all my teachers,
for I meditate on your statutes. (verse 99)
I have more understanding than the elders,
for I obey your precepts. (verse 100)
Great peace have they who love your law,
and nothing can make them stumble. (verse 165)

8

PRIORITIES

what matters most?

Have you ever noticed that some people seem to be enormously productive, despite the fact that their days have 24 hours in them, the same as the rest of us? They just seem to be able to cram more in, or get more out of, those same 24 hours.

I think that the family behind the popular girl-band BarlowGirl is like that. Rebecca, Alyssa, and Lauren Barlow are the musicians, singers, and songwriters that comprise the group. In addition to teaching them to play their instruments years ago, their dad, Vincent, now manages the group. This wonderfully productive Christian ministry is a successful family affair.

Let me tell you how I saw the family members' working relationships up close.

Q AND A WITH BARLOWGIRL

By the devilish look in the young man's eyes, I should have known that he was going to ask something off the wall.

It was an open-mic question-and-answer session in front of about a thousand teens. The event was Spirit West Coast, a major Christian event held in California. For the second year in a row, I had the privilege of moderating a question-and-answer session with BarlowGirl. Dozens of teens stood in line to ask sisters Rebecca, Alyssa, and Lauren questions about everything from "How can I get into the music biz" to "How do you each maintain your daily devotions while on tour?"

As the emcee I was the liaison between the audience and the stage. Sometimes I would interject a thought when the conversation lagged momentarily. One of the last young men who approached the mic had a big smile on his face when he asked the group, "If I come up onstage, will any one of you give me a kiss?"

The audience howled with laughter, the young man blushed, and Vince Barlow rushed up to me, grabbed the mic, and said to the audience, "Alex, let me handle this question!"

It was pretty funny. The Q-and-A session gave the audience a glimpse into the lives of three busy Christian musicians, and one young man caught a glimpse of a cordial (but protective) Christian dad!

Putting God first in their lives

When members of the band Superchick met Rebecca, Alyssa, and Lauren at a concert several years ago, they were so impressed by the sisters' commitment to godly living that they recorded a song about them called "Barlow Girl." I, too, was deeply impressed with the girls' faithfulness to their beliefs: sexual abstinence before marriage, always dressing modestly, and choosing to live at home and not pursue the dating scene.

Clearly the Barlow sisters are serious about their walk and witness. And besides being deeply committed, consistent followers of Jesus Christ, the sisters are involved in the nonstop activities that go with being pop stars. It is very impressive to see young adults who are driven to live their lives in accord with God's priorities. BarlowGirl is proof that one can make a big-time mark for Jesus without compromising the things that the Bible says are important.

WHERE IS YOUR HEART INVESTED?

Let's face it. We invest ourselves in the things we think are important. For the Christian, priorities should be chosen and nurtured in light of God's Words. Keeping your priorities in line with what God says is important and can spare you from much of life's anguish.

Why is it so important that your goals, desires,

A tough choice

Barry Collins is an owner and operator of a machine shop and metal-working company in his home state of North Carolina. During the 1980s tough economic times hit. The Christmas holidays were approaching, and opportunities for new work had trickled away to almost nothing. Barry asked God to send some jobs so he wouldn't have to lay off workers.

A few days before Christmas, a man came in with a folder of mechanical drawings. Could Barry's machine shop create these complicated parts? Could the men make these precision items accurately and quickly? Barry's answers were "yes" and "yes!" The project would bring in several thousands dollars and would tide things over financially until the New Year rolled around. "By the way," Barry asked, "what type of machine are these parts for?"

It turned out the parts were for a large beer manufacturer. The man's next words hit Barry's tender heart like a dagger: "Your creation of these parts will help us ship more beer to more people, and faster!"

The company needed money, but Barry told the

attitudes, and life in general always be surrendered to God's will? Why should all of your plans be checked to make sure they are in alignment with Scripture? The answer is very simple: God knows best. The Lord Jesus cares for you with a divine, supernatural love, and He has special plans for every life. Plus, God's great design for your life is coupled with the power to actually bring such things to pass. Let me be clear: A relationship with God is the only thing man that as a christian his conscience would not allow him to help make beer faster for more people. The money problem was not solved, but Barry's conscience was clear. As Barry prepared to leave the building, he knew that the next day he would have to break bad news to the men who would be laid off. "God, I trust you," he prayed. "Please show me what to do."

Just then a voice called out, "Is anyone still here? Are you still open?" A major company that produced interiors for commercial airlines had heard of Barry's company. Even though it was past five o'clock, the man had come by in hopes of catching someone still in the office. The company wanted Barry's men to make parts for airplane interiors. It would be a contract that was both long term and highly profitable. Ultimately no machinists were laid off! Barry's men worked through Christmas and for many years afterward.

Barry's faithfulness in honoring God's priorities resulted in greater and more long-term blessings. Following God is like that—not always easy, but always right.

you've got in life that can't be taken away.

Let's look at how our intentions and actions integrate into a prioritized Christian life.

Intentions

Good intentions are important. The psalm writer proclaims his love for the Law and for God throughout Psalm 119. "My soul is consumed with longing for your laws at all times," we read in verse 20.

Good intentions are our starting point in aligning our priorities with God's priorities. We must learn that our ways are not as good as God's ways. As verse 2 says, "Blessed are they who . . . seek him with all their heart."

Actions

Good intentions, however, are not enough. You may have heard the old saying: "priorities are what you do. The rest is just talk." Janet Folger, a Christian activist who has written a number of excellent books, has given this old saying a spiritual twist. She says, "Faith is what you do. The rest is just religious talk."

She's right. If you believe in something, you act. Let's look at a story found in Luke 14:1-6. On a Sabbath day, Jesus went to eat at the home of a prominent Pharisee. A man with a disease was there too. The Pharisees there were experts in the Law, and they had given the invitation to Jesus as a trap. They wanted to see if Jesus would heal the man on the Sabbath, which they thought was against God's Law. Sure enough, Jesus healed the man because He had pure intentions—love for the suffering man. He acted in faith and healed

Tell me where you spend your time and money, and there you'll find your heart.

the man on the Sabbath. Jesus brought the law of love—the true spirit of Psalm 119 and all of the rest of the Law—to life.

Integration

When something is completely destroyed, we have
a word for that: disintegrated. And what is the op-
posite of disintegrated? Integrated. When something is fully integrated, all the parts work together
appropriately and effectively.

Have you ever noticed that the English words *integrity* and *integrated* are similar? That's no accident. We think of integrity as a character quality.
We talk about a person who has integrity. Such a
person is honest and straightforward. He (or she)
will do what he says and will act with honor.

We sometimes, though, speak of things—inani-
mate objects—as having integrity. A strong bridge,
for example, is said to have structural integrity. But
have you ever seen a suspension bridge, such as
San Francisco's Golden Gate Bridge or New York
City's George Washington Bridge? Some of the cables pull to the left, and some pull to the right.
Some cables sag and sway from tower to tower, and
some are taut from top to bottom. From a distance
a suspension bridge looks impossibly frail. But because all these cables counterbalance one another,
the bridge is enormously strong. It has structural
integrity.

At the beginning of this story, I told you how all
the elements of Rebecca, Alyssa, and Lauren Barlow's
lives are integrated. They have crafted their lives in
such a way that most everything they do points them
in the direction they believe God wants them to go.

In what direction is God pointing you? What is

God's overarching purpose for you? In a way, we are all bridges. We are at a certain place in life, but God would not have us end up where we start out. He tells us to grow and to serve. Where is the other end of your bridge, and how are you going to get there? When you know the answer to that question, you can begin to align your priorities and to live a truly integrated life.

Priorities of a Christian

Oh, that my ways were steadfast
in obeying your decrees! (verse 5)
I will praise you with an upright heart
as I learn your righteous laws. (verse 7)
I meditate on your precepts
and consider your ways. (verse 15)
I recounted my ways and you answered me;
teach me your decrees. (verse 26)
I will never forget your precepts,
for by them you have preserved my life. (verse 93)
Though I constantly take my life in my hands,
I will not forget your law. (verse 109)
My heart is set on keeping your decrees
to the very end. (verse 112)
I hate double-minded men,
but I love your law. (verse 113)
I have kept my feet from every evil path
so that I might obey your word. (verse 101)
I have not departed from your laws,

for you yourself have taught me. (verse 102)

I gain understanding from your precepts;

therefore I hate every wrong path. (verse 104)

My eyes fail, looking for your salvation,

looking for your righteous promise. (verse 123)

Deal with your servant according to your love

and teach me your decrees. (verse 124)

I am your servant; give me discernment

that I may understand your statutes. (verse 125)

Direct my footsteps according to your word;

let no sin rule over me. (verse 133)

9

TROUBLES

God's words in times of adversity

Is your life perfect and trouble-free?

I know. It's a ridiculous question. None of us have perfect, trouble-free lives. Indeed, part of being human is living in a world that is less than perfect, with people who are less than perfect. Ecclesiastes tells us that we "eat our bread in sorrow." That is the reality of the human condition.

The writer of Psalm 119 knows about trouble. He says he has been attacked by the "arrogant" (verses 21, 51, 69). He says he was "afflicted" (verses 67, 71). Yet when we read Psalm 119, we don't think of it as a tale of woe. Indeed, by this point in our discussion, we can see that Psalm 119 is a tale of triumph. It is a book about the power, strength, and eternal nature of God and His Words.

Is it therefore possible that our weakness and God's strength are somehow related? The answer to that is a resounding yes.

TROUBLES TEACH RIGHTEOUSNESS

It is important to remember that God neither promises us, nor requires of us, a trouble-free life. What he requires of us are obedience and righteousness. But because we are sinful, it is often troubles—which are nothing more than the consequences of sin in the world—that lead us back to God.

Fancy word alert: Reductionism means that a complex argument has been "reduced." In apologetics, reductionism is trying to distort the facts.

It might be logical to ask: If God is all-powerful, then why doesn't He just make us obedient and righteous? That's a simple enough solution; He would get what He wants, and we would get what we need.

But like many simple answers, it is incomplete. In other words, it solves only part of the problem and not the whole problem. Remember, we were made in God's own image. That means, in part, that we have the ability to choose. You see, God not only wants us to be righteous; He wants us to choose righteousness.

TROUBLES MAKE PLAIN GOD'S MERCY

How can that be? How can being in trouble be a good thing?

Consider this: Ideas and the behaviors that spring from them have consequences. Those consequences are determined by God's laws and are based on God's character. To use a simple example, consider what happens when you throw a rock off a bridge. Does that rock fly? Of course not. It will fall to the river below. If you hired a motivational speaker to tell the rock that it could fly, the law of gravity would still win. That rock would still fall into the river. Why? Because on this planet and all others, gravity is universal and inevitable.

God's laws are also universal and inevitable. If we persist in breaking His laws, the ultimate consequences are eternally catastrophic. God shows us mercy by allowing barriers to be put in our way to keep that from happening. Said another way, God loves us so much that He gives us the ability to choose, but He has given us laws and precepts that point us toward making the right choices. Right choices result in joy and intimacy with God. Bad choices result in trouble. Over time we learn to make more right choices and fewer bad choices. That is God's mercy at work in our lives. Verse 71 puts it this way: "It was good for me to be afflicted so that I might learn your decrees."

THE PROBLEM OF EVIL, THE POWER OF JESUS

So troubles teach Christ's character. But Jesus encountered troubles, and He was perfect. How do you explain that? Great question. Here's the difficult answer: evil.

Evil is as real, more powerful, than the physical

Think you've got troubles?

Even the most dedicated Christians have problems—there's no way around them. Look what
the apostle Paul faced: He said, "I have worked
much harder [than a 'super-Christian'], been in
prison more frequently, been flogged more se-
verely, and been exposed to death again and
again. Five times I received from the Jews the
forty lashes minus one. Three times I was beaten
with rods, once I was stoned, three times I was
shipwrecked, I spent a night and a day in the
open sea, I have been constantly on the move.

world around us. We must never forget that we are
in the midst of a spiritual universe, which is in the
midst of a spiritual battle. The struggles we face
are part of the "collateral damage" of the Fall and
will continue until Christ returns in triumph.

One of the most important things to realize
about humans is that we
are made in God's image.
This means, first and foremost, that we have a spiritual life that is eternal. This
life, it has been said, is
mere preparation for the
next life. Evil exists in this world. God didn't create
evil, but He allows it. What He did create for us is
the ability to choose. Jesus demonstrated His power
over evil by always and in every circumstance making the right choices. He always chose God over evil.

*The writer refers to
himself 325 times in
Psalm 119. Of these,
66 contain references
to personal suffering.*

I have been in danger from rivers, in danger
from bandits, in danger from my own country-
men, in danger from Gentiles; in danger in the
city, in danger in the country, in danger at sea;
and in danger from false brothers. I have la-
bored and toiled and have often gone without
sleep; I have known hunger and thirst and have
often gone without food; I have been cold and
naked. Besides everything else, I face daily the
pressure of my concern for all the churches"
(2 Corinthians 11:23-28).

So in a very real sense, Jesus' encounters with
evil and with Satan were done on our behalf. They
are proof of His divinity, and of His ability to do
what He said He would do, namely, to take upon
Himself the sins of the world.

THE WAY HOME

Most boys of my generation were fascinated by the
space program. So I can't help but recount here an
episode from the Apollo era that brings into sharp
focus some of what we've been discussing in this
chapter about troubles.

In 1970 the Apollo 13 spacecraft was in real
trouble. It was so damaged by an explosion in
the oxygen tank that the likelihood of getting the
astronauts home was slim to none. In a complicated
life-and-death dilemma, Commander Jim Lovell

notified NASA with the simple statement, "Houston, we've had a problem." This quote has become one of the most famous single lines in American history. The understated calm of that statement became a symbol for grace under fire.

A great movie was based on this episode. One scene depicts a news network that decided to broadcast an interview with Lovell that was taped before blastoff. Lovell said he was once flying a mission in Southeast Asia when his radar went out and his fuel was running low. It was pitch black below, and he had no way of finding his aircraft carrier. That's big trouble. But then, things got worse. Not only did he lose his radar, but even the lights in his cockpit went out. He couldn't tell how much fuel he had or even if his engine was running properly.

But a remarkable thing happened. So long as he had cockpit lights, his eyes could not fully adjust to the night. But when the power failed completely, he looked up and out. He could see stars, and more important, he could see the millions of phosphorescent sea creatures that had been stirred up by the propeller of his aircraft carrier. They formed a pale green path that led directly to his ship—and safety. Lovell said, "Sometimes when you think things can't get any worse, they do, but that may be just what needs to happen to lead you home."

So let us not fear troubles or wish them away. God allows them in our lives so we will turn to Him or submit to Him more completely. Never forget that this life is not all there is. God certainly knows that, and He is preparing us for eternity even when we ourselves are focused on much more local, proximate concerns. The TROUBLES in our lives—even the ones you think are simply too much to bear— might be the very ones God has allowed to lead us home—to Him.

Psalm 119 on trouble and adversity

Before I was afflicted I went astray,
but now I obey your word. (verse 67)
It was good for me to be afflicted
so that I might learn your decrees. (verse 71)
My soul faints with longing for your salvation,
but I have put my hope in your word. (verse 81)
My eyes fail, looking for your promise;
I say, "When will you comfort me?" (verse 82)
Though I am like a wineskin in the smoke,
I do not forget your decrees. (verse 83)
All your commands are trustworthy;
help me, for men persecute me without cause. (verse 86)
They almost wiped me from the earth,
but I have not forsaken your precepts. (verse 87)
If your law had not been my delight,
I would have perished in my affliction. (verse 92)
The wicked are waiting to destroy me,
but I will ponder your statutes. (verse 95)
Streams of tears flow from my eyes,

for your law is not obeyed. (verse 136)
My zeal wears me out,
for my enemies ignore your words. (verse 139)
Trouble and distress have come upon me,
but your commands are my delight. (verse 143)

10

ATTITUDE

the perspective of a godly mind

Americans are, generally, an optimistic people with a go-get-'em attitude. American popular literature is full of exhortations to be optimistic. And since a protestant pastor, Norman Vincent Peale, wrote *The Power of Positive Thinking* in the 1950s, positive thinking has increasingly become a part of American religious thought as well. "Your attitude, not your aptitude, determines your altitude," said self-help guru Zig Ziglar. Today, writers such as Joel Osteen continue in that tradition with books like *Your Best Life Now*. They're designed to make us feel better about ourselves, to have a better self-image, and to overcome the obstacles before us.

Don't get me wrong. I'm a big believer in having a positive mental attitude. People who know me call me an upbeat, optimistic person. But when I talk about attitude in this chapter, I'm not talking about feeling better about myself. I'm upbeat

Armed with a positive attitude

Daniel Ritchie is a friend who reminds me to be thankful for God's blessings. Let me tell you about him. I first saw him when he was about five. Daniel was a tiny little boy then, running around with all of the other children at our church christmas party. Next I think of Daniel's teen years, as all of us watched him grow up and become a deeply devoted christian. Daniel seemed to be wise beyond his years. He had a warmth about him that impressed me. In high school, Daniel told me that he felt God was calling him to full-time christian ministry. He later attended seminary, graduated from a rigorous academic program, and shortly after graduation got married. Today Daniel lives in Arizona, where he ministers to

not because I think I'm so great but because God is so great, and He has saved me from myself! It's no accident, as we have discussed throughout this book, that the Bible uses the words *blessed* and *happy* interchangeably. Happiness is not an emotion. It is a condition of the mind and heart when you are living in and with and under God's blessing. When we accept God's blessings for us, happiness is the inevitable result.

The problem today is that people seek this happiness in all kinds of other ways. Some of the ways we pursue happiness, such as the "positive thinking" techniques, are not perhaps as bad as seeking happiness in alcohol, drugs, pornography, or promiscuity. But neither are they completely harmless.

youth and college students as assistant pastor of a thriving church.

We all meet people who love the Lord, so why does Daniel Ritchie make such a lasting impression? Well, the images I have of him—a rough and tumble little boy, a godly teen, a faithful young minister—all become more and more impressive when you learn that Daniel was born without arms.

But does he feel sorry for himself? Is he mad at God? No, and no. His attitude more than compensates for any physical limitations. That's why he inspires me so much to love Jesus and serve to the best of my ability. I wish I could fulfill my role with the same zeal that Daniel shows.

After all, most alcoholics and drug addicts know something is not right. They know the numbness or euphoria they feel is temporary and in fact does not solve the underlying problems in their lives. But positive-thinking disciples may come to believe that their problems *are* solved, that they are "good" and need only to recognize that goodness in themselves. This is a dangerous position to take because it might seduce us into thinking we do not need a Savior.

Years ago the founder of Campus Crusade for Christ, Bill Bright, wrote an evangelistic tract called the *Four Spiritual Laws.* That simple little booklet had a memorable illustration of a train with three cars. The locomotive is labeled "fact."

The passenger car is labeled "faith." Finally, the caboose is labeled "feeling."

The problem with most preachers and teachers who espouse the positive-thinking philosophy is that they don't take into account the hard, cold fact of our sinfulness.

There might be some positive-thinking disciples who think this idea is a real downer, a killjoy. But it is not. In fact, it is the only solid ground on which you can stand as you climb upward toward a truly positive attitude—which is an attitude based on reality and God's truth.

ATTITUDE AND THE TRUTH

As a Christian apologist I tend to think about all issues, all ideas, in relation to God's eternal truth. So when I hear people say they are not happy, or they want to be happy, or they want to have a "positive attitude," my tendency is to say, "Well, what does Scripture say about that?"

I have already made the point that happiness, or blessedness, is a condition of the soul but not of the emotions. The person who is happy is the person who has a right relationship to the truth. Let me explain what I mean by that.

In the previous chapter I talked about how many boys were gripped by the space program when I was growing up. Watching those early telecasts of moon shots may have been where I first heard the word attitude, but it had nothing to do with feelings, positive or negative. In the language of space flight, the "attitude" of a body in flight is its position and direction in relationship to a certain frame of reference. Attitude control is one of the most basic problems of space flight. After all, consider what it means to launch a spacecraft to the moon. You need to aim the rocket where the moon will be, not where the moon is now. And you also have to keep in mind that the platform from which you are launching, the earth, is spinning around the sun at 35,000 miles per hour. And coming back to earth is even more complicated because of the earth's atmosphere. If the spaceship comes back too fast, or too steeply, it burns up in the atmosphere. If the spaceship's attitude is too shallow, it skips off the atmosphere like a stone skips off water. In either case, the ship and its inhabitants are doomed.

My point is this: In the spiritual realm, as in the physical realm, attitude has a definite relationship to absolute, immutable laws. Space engineers don't have the luxury of saying, "We'll just turn off gravity for a few minutes during the re-entry process, because that will make everything a bit easier to deal with." Neither can we turn off the "spiritual gravity" of God's Law. But it's also important to understand that if we truly looked at things from God's perspective, we wouldn't *want* to turn off His Law. As I have already mentioned, God's

Law protects us and guides us. God's Law directs us toward God Himself. Grace does not turn off God's Law. Grace fulfills God's Law.

So what does it mean to have the proper attitude? First and foremost, it means having a proper attitude toward God and His Law. That means having the proper position and the proper perspective.

Attitudes of a godly mind

My soul is consumed with longing
for your laws at all times. (verse 20)
You rebuke the arrogant, who are cursed
and who stray from your commands. (verse 21)
My soul is weary with sorrow;
strengthen me according to your word. (verse 28)
My comfort in my suffering is this:
Your promise preserves my life. (verse 50)
Indignation grips me because of the wicked,
who have forsaken your law. (verse 53)
Their hearts are callous and unfeeling,
but I delight in your law. (verse 70)
It was good for me to be afflicted
so that I might learn your decrees. (verse 71)
The law from your mouth is more precious to me
than thousands of pieces of silver and gold. (verse 72)

11

GOALS

avoiding spiritual land mines

We are a results-obsessed culture. We measure everything. For example, within minutes of being born, an infant is weighed, measured, and given an Apgar test, which scores its breathing, heart rate, color, muscle tone, and reflexes. In preschool, children are tested on their social skills, color awareness, and ability to recognize letters. In Sunday school, stars are given to those children who attend, to those who bring Bibles, and to those who memorize their verses. In school, the grading in all subjects begins in elementary school and ends in high school with a final class rank, GPA, and SAT score.

Having goals is a good thing. Measuring results also has its place. The Bible is not indifferent to numbers. In fact, one of the 66 books of the Bible is even called Numbers!

But we must be careful when we select goals for ourselves. There is an old saying that goes like this: "Be careful what you ask for, for you shall surely get it." If we let the world define our goals, those goals are likely to be of the kind we have already mentioned. We might make more money, lose more weight, play better at sports, or have newer and better things—but are these the goals God wants for us?

I think the answer to that question is no. That's why when I talk about life goals, what I'm really talking about is this: How do we seek the goals God has for us?

THE SPIRITUAL LAND MINES BETWEEN US AND OUR GOALS

In a goal-oriented, success-obsessed culture, it is tempting even for Christians to express our goals in those terms. We talk about having an "impact" on our world for Christ. We want to be part of a kingdom movement or a revolution for Jesus. In other words, even in the Christian world, we measure our worth based on performance rather than our identity in Christ. Keep in mind, however, that whatever we *do* for Jesus will eventually pass away. Who we *are* is what matters to God. As I speak around the country, I use this expression to capture that idea: What is internal is what is eternal.

No matter how well intentioned we are when we

select our performance goals, it is important to remember that the One who spoke the universe into existence from nothingness doesn't really need anything we can do for Him.

God wants us to love Him, to enjoy Him (take our complete satisfaction in Him and nothing else), and to glorify Him.

God loves us not for what we can do for Him but for what we are in Him.

But the world, our own flesh, and the Devil conspire to get us to forget these simple goals. That's why leaning daily on the Words of God is so important. Psalm 119 shows us how to get around spiritual land mines.

Land mine No. 1: Circumstances that look hopeless

In chapter 9 I told you the story of pilot Jim Lovell's flight mission in Southeast Asia and how a bad situation had to become even worse before he could find his way home. The truth is, God often works that way. We so often refuse to follow God's ways that He lets us follow our own goals—until we get ourselves in a place of hopelessness where we have to trust Him. So don't despair when things seem hopeless; just look to God. And, by the way, learn from that situation. True wisdom comes from trusting God *before* things become hopeless. Psalm 119's advice is this: "My soul faints with longing for your salvation, but I have put my hope in your word" (verse 81).

Baaah!

okay, get used to it. The Bible calls us sheep. on a good hair day, sheep are tolerably attractive. And considering their brainless behavior and penchant for doing the same silly things over and over and over and over, sheep make a sorry symbol for humanity. using sheep as a representation for humans reveals that, by biblical standards, we are stupid and helpless. we need someone to come after us, to bring us back to a safe place, to be our shepherd.

For more scripture sheepishness see Numbers 27:16-17; Psalms 23; 44; 79:13; 100:3; Isaiah 53:6; Jeremiah 23:1; 50:6; Ezekiel 34:11-31; Micah 2:12; Matthew 9:36; 18:12-14; John 10.

Land mine No. 2: Squandered time, money, or opportunity

Before I became a Christian, I played guitar in a bar band. One night I got drunk, and my so-called friends threw me in a trash Dumpster. I awoke on Saturday morning with rotting garbage all over me. That experience was a turning point in my life. It was a low point from which I was powerless to raise myself, but that experience forced me to set my goals to please God instead of myself.

Even after I had turned toward God, I was racked by guilt over wasted time, money, and opportunities. But over the years God has shown me how He can redeem the "years the locusts have eaten," as the Old Testament prophet Joel said (Joel 2:25). He did that in my life by giving me a sense of urgency that I might not have had otherwise. Also, one of the greatest temptations for a Christian worker is spiritual pride. Sometimes after speaking at a teen event that seems to have impacted people or after I've discussed one of my books on a television program, I am tempted to say, "Look what I'm doing for God!" But the memory of waking up in that Dumpster reminds me that it is God who is at work. Those old memories no longer condemn me, but they do remind me who is really in control. Psalm 119's take is this: "I have strayed like a lost sheep. Seek your servant, for I have not forgotten your commands" (verse 176).

Land mine No. 3: Responsibilities that seem futile

Before he retired after a successful career, author Hyler Bracey used to own a successful consulting company. He regularly told his employees, "I want you to love your job, and I'll work with you to make sure that we create a work environment that creates that feeling in you as many days as possible. But I also know that no matter how hard we both work at this goal, there will be days when you won't love your job. On those days, I just want you to *do* your job."

The Christian life is like that. Living life with God brings great satisfaction and joy. And most days it's fun. But we live in a fallen world. We can't always see the end result of our work, even our work for God. But never forget that God has a purpose for things that seem futile. Michael Omartian, a great Christian musician and record producer, thanked his piano teacher for making him practice when he didn't want to. Omartian had great talent, but it was his mastery of the fundamentals of music—sight-reading, scales, and other musical theory—that made him a popular session player and producer.

Whatever responsibilities God has put before you, do carry them out with all the diligence and excellence you can muster. These responsibilities—and your response to them—are preparing you for something great. A godly goal is to do everything as if for the Lord. "My heart is set on keeping your decrees to the very end" (verse 112).

Land mine No. 4: Questions that seem to have no answers

As a Christian apologist I'm in the business of providing answers to tough questions about the faith. After more than 20 years of this work, there are a couple of things I can say about questions that seem to have no answers.

First, most questions have answers, good answers. I hate to say it so bluntly, but the truth is that most people are either too lazy or too committed to their own way of viewing things to seek the answers. Now, if you have nagging questions about faith, I realize that this probably seems judgmental at worst or unhelpful at best. I don't mean to be either. But if you have tough questions, I would ask this: Have you struggled diligently in prayer and consulted Scripture, good books, and with thoughtful people about these questions? If not, I would recommend these as first steps.

Second, I do have this confession to make. Some questions really don't have good answers—at least not for us, here and now. We humans are finite. We are made in God's image, but we are not God. All of the understanding of all of our wisest men amounts to only an inkling of the infinite and the eternal. It is at this point where faith comes into play. But God doesn't ask us to take a leap of faith, only a step of faith. He asks us to walk as far as we can by sight and then take one more step in that same direction—by faith.

And is that so strange? After all, I don't understand how my computer works, but that doesn't mean it doesn't work. I don't understand what my mechanic does to fix my car. But because he has fixed many thousands of cars and because he has fixed mine time after time, I now trust him. If we are willing to trust other fallible human beings with questions to which we do not know the answers, why should we not trust a God who has proven Himself faithful and loving time and time again throughout history?

A godly goal is to diligently seek God's wisdom

and yet trust Him when those answers seem elusive in this lifetime. Psalm 119 encourages, "Let me understand the teaching of your precepts; then I will meditate on your wonders" (verse 27).

Land mine No. 5: Dreams that may not have come true

God put you here for a specific purpose. I think many of us have a sense of that. We have dreams that we believe God has given us. And when those dreams don't come true, the emotional pain can be crushing.

But let me tell you that I cannot think of a single person who has been used mightily by God who has not been broken, has not had his or her dreams crushed at least once. It is not that God delights in seeing our dreams crushed, but He does delight in His children pursuing His will, and we are sometimes so stubborn that we will pursue our own dreams no matter what. Many of Jesus' disciples had in their minds that He would be an earthly king. They had a dream for Jesus and for themselves that did not involve the humiliation of the cross.

Sometimes we need to thank God for dreams that didn't come true. Our wants and desires need to be constantly evaluated in light of God's authority over us. Even the writer of Psalm 119 had crushed dreams, but he looked to God for help: "I am laid low in the dust; preserve my life according to your word" (verse 25).

MY GOAL FOR YOU

The main goal I have for this book is to encourage you to read God's Words more often, beginning with Psalm 119. There is an undeniable correlation between one's spiritual health and the role the Bible plays in a Christian's day-to-day life. Regarding this, Dwight L. Moody (one of my heroes of church history) wrote this in *Pleasures and Profit in Bible Study*:

> I prayed for Faith, and I thought that someday Faith would come down and strike me like lightning. But Faith did not come. One day I was reading the tenth chapter of Romans: "Faith cometh by hearing, and hearing by the Word of God" [verse 17]. I had closed my Bible, and prayed for Faith. I now opened my Bible, and began to study, and Faith has been growing ever since.

If you want your faith in God to become stronger, spend time reading God's Words on a consistent basis.

Billy Graham and Charles Templeton

The importance of allowing the Bible to influence your life is illustrated by the life of evangelist Dr. Billy Graham. As I am writing this book, Charlotte, North Carolina, is gearing up to celebrate his 90th birthday. Every day the newspaper is running articles about his life and its impact on Christian ministry around the world. One article estimated that in more than six decades of ministry, Dr. Graham spoke live to 250 million people. Amazing! God used Billy Graham in a myriad of ways, yet the preacher has remained humble about it all. In the newspaper coverage about Dr. Graham's life, he remarked that if he could live his life all over again, he wishes he had invested more time in studying. He said that he would like to have spent more time reading good books, especially his Bible. Dr. Graham said he had never met a Christian who got off track and really knew his or her Bible.

In the 1950s Dr. Graham traveled with another up-and-coming minister, Charles Templeton. Those people who heard them agree that Templeton was the more impressive of the two evangelists. However, the men's lives ultimately charted different courses. Billy Graham spent six decades attempting to reach every corner of the globe with the gospel. Templeton walked away from the ministry, from his Christian faith, and eventually declared himself an atheist.

What made the difference in their spiritual lives? The answer is how each viewed the Bible. Charles Templeton approached God's Word with suspicion, questioning its validity, and he finally rejected its content altogether. Instead of passing judgment on the Bible, Billy Graham allowed the Bible to judge *him*.

Of course, it's not wrong to have questions about

Scripture. Ask the tough questions but be willing to seek the answers and submit to the Words of God in all areas of life. The ultimate results of life arise from the choices we each make about God. Remember that He speaks to us through circumstances, through other people, and in a variety of other ways, but mainly through His Words. I encourage you to set the goal of making His Words a significant and daily part of your journey. You can start with the reading guide in the following chapter.

Goals for the godly

I run in the path of your commands,
for you have set my heart free. (verse 32)
Teach me, O Lord, to follow your decrees;
then I will keep them to the end. (verse 33)
Give me understanding, and I will keep your law
and obey it with all my heart. (verse 34)
I will always obey your law,
for ever and ever. (verse 44)
I will walk about in freedom,
for I have sought out your precepts. (verse 45)
Teach me knowledge and good judgment,
for I believe in your commands. (verse 66)
May my heart be blameless toward your decrees,
that I may not be put to shame. (verse 80)
I have taken an oath and confirmed it,
that I will follow your righteous laws. (verse 106)

A PSALM 119 READING GUIDE

precious jewels from God's words

The Asian republic of Sri Lanka has often been called the pearl of the Indian Ocean. Certain rivers that run through this island nation certainly live up to that name. The sands of the riverbeds contain large deposits of rubies, sapphires, garnets, mica, and beautiful types of quartz. Legends say that King Solomon imported jewels from Sri Lanka to impress the Queen of Sheba. The gemstones were supposedly plentiful enough to have made many of the ancient pirates jealous!

Psalm 119:72 says, "The law from your mouth is more precious to me than thousands of pieces of silver and gold." Sure, being able to scoop up handfuls of gemstones from a river would be impressive. But more meaningful than that is the opportunity to daily open God's Word and receive jewels off of every page. You can tell where the priorities were for the one who wrote this psalm. He saw God's Words as having more value than any human unit of currency. For sure, God's Words are *priceless*.

Follow this daily reading guide to find out what jewels might be found in Psalm 119. Each group of

verses is named after a letter of the Hebrew alphabet. On the lines, write down a personal reflection
or "jewel" to think about or meditate on.

Day 1—Aleph

Verses 1-8

_____

_____

_____

_____

Day 2—Beth

Verses 9-16

_____

_____

_____

_____

Day 3—Gimel

Verses 17-24

_____

_____

_____

_____

_____

Day 4—Daleth

Verses 25-32

_____

_____

_____

_____

_____

Day 5—He

Verses 33-40

_____

_____

_____

_____

_____

Day 6—Waw

Verses 41-48

_____

_____

_____

_____

_____

Day 7—Zayin

Verses 49-56

_____

_____

_____

_____

_____

Day 8—Heth

Verses 57-64

_____

_____

_____

_____

_____

Day 9—Teth

Verses 65-72

_____

_____

_____

_____

_____

Day 10—Yodh

Verses 73-80

_____

_____

_____

_____

_____

Day 11—Kaph

Verses 81-88

_____

_____

_____

_____

_____

Day 12—Lamedh

Verses 89-96

_____

_____

_____

_____

_____

Day 13—Mem

Verses 97-104

_____

_____

_____

_____

_____

Day 14—Nun

Verses 105-112

_____

_____

_____

_____

_____

Day 15—Samekh

Verses 113-120

_____

_____

_____

_____

_____

Day 16—Ayin

Verses 121-128

_____

_____

_____

_____

_____

Day 17—Pe

Verses 129-136

_____

_____

_____

_____

_____

Day 18—Tsadhe

Verses 137-144

_____

_____

_____

_____

_____

Day 19—Qoph

Verses 145-152

_____

_____

_____

_____

_____

Day 20—Resh

Verses 153-160

_____

_____

_____

_____

_____

Day 21—Sin and Shin

Verses 161-168

_____

_____

_____

_____

_____

Day 22—Taw

Verses 169-176

_____

_____

_____

_____

_____

Focus on the Family's The Truth Project® Presents

Is your faith ready for real life?
Introducing TrueU™—a revolutionary DVD
series that will challenge your worldview,
strengthen your foundations and show you
what it really takes to stay strong in college.

Order at FocusOnTheFamily.com/resources

FOCUS ^{ON}_{THE} FAMILY®

Welcome to the Family

Whether you purchased this book, borrowed it, or received it as a gift, we're glad you're reading it. It's just one of the many helpful, encouraging, and biblically based resources produced by Focus on the Family® for people in all stages of life.

Focus began in 1977 with the vision of one man, Dr. James Dobson, a licensed psychologist and author of numerous best-selling books on marriage, parenting, and family. Alarmed by the societal, political, and economic pressures that were threatening the existence of the American family, Dr. Dobson founded Focus on the Family with one employee and a once-a-week radio broadcast aired on 36 stations.

Now an international organization reaching millions of people daily, Focus on the Family is dedicated to preserving values and strengthening and encouraging families through the life-changing message of Jesus Christ.

Focus on the Family MAGAZINES

These faith-building, character-developing publications address the interests, issues, concerns, and challenges faced by every member of your family from preschool through the senior years.

For More INFORMATION

ONLINE:
Log on to
FocusOnTheFamily.com
In Canada, log on to
FocusOnTheFamily.ca

PHONE:
Call toll-free:
800-A-FAMILY
(232-6459)
In Canada, call toll-free:
800-661-9800

FOCUS ON THE FAMILY® MAGAZINE	FOCUS ON THE FAMILY CLUBHOUSE JR.® Ages 4 to 8	FOCUS ON THE FAMILY CLUBHOUSE® Ages 8 to 12	FOCUS ON THE FAMILY CITIZEN® U.S. news issues

Rev. 12/08

More Great Resources
from Focus on the Family®

More Great Resources
from Focus on the Family®

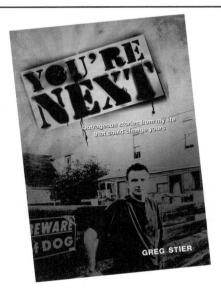

You're Next:
Outrageous Stories from My Life
that Could Change Yours
by Greg Stier

Like many teens, Greg grappled with big questions about God . . . only how he arrived at answers was anything but normal. Truth made Greg a crazy man for God—and *You're Next*! These outrageous true stories will give you a taste of God's extreme love, which just might spread to your friends, family, and even strangers. Paperback.